DANCE IN THE SUN

DANCE IN THE SUN

BEING THE AUTHENTIC YOU

Monique Moliere Piper

Piper & Piper

Publishing

DANCE IN THE SUN
BEING THE AUTHENTIC YOU

PUBLISHED BY PIPER & PIPER PUBLISHING
NEW ORLEANS, LA

ISBN: 978-0-6157-3560-3

This book is dedicated to

Timothy, my loving husband who supports me even in moments he has no idea what I am doing.

To **mother,** you taught me no dream was too big to dream.

To **Joshua, Christian,** and **Alanna** my 3 gifts from God. You inspire me to be a better mother and person every day I am blessed to witness the sun shine.

To **Adrieanne** aka Dredabird my baby sister. Thank you for being the beautiful light in our family.

TABLE OF CONTENTS

~ INTRODUCTION ~
Strategies to Get Through It All

L et me begin by saying: if you picked up this book looking to read a larger-than-life story, close the book right this minute and keep browsing the aisle. No, this is not some type of reverse psychology to lure you into buying this book – it's the truth. There are literally thousands of books out there that will give you exactly what you want. I have read some of them myself, that's how I'm sure this book does not fit the bill.

I am an ordinary woman seeking to live what has become, for many of us, an extraordinary life. Extraordinary only because living in an authentic space is largely uncommon. This is a space where you are free to become who you were meant to be, instead of who you were conditioned to be, or who you believe you cannot be because of bright red stop signs…painted by YOU.

We have become a disorderly bunch suppressed by outside expectations and inside limitations.

Dance in the Sun is about getting started on the journey to living exactly as God created us all to be, our authentic selves. It addresses the ways in which this journey gets constantly interrupted by our habits, beliefs, and conditioning and the struggles in our lives that cloud our view so that we never catch a glimpse of our true selves. This book will show you ways to get on the path to uncovering your heart's desires, instead of what you have been taught is realistic.

I use parts of my own life to illustrate how we become disconnected from our real desires. Sometimes, we can become disconnected to the point of virtual amnesia, forgetting what brings us real joy and true happiness, rather than fleeting good moods. We are simply reacting to whatever comes our way because we fail to consciously direct our lives, believing that much of what occurs on the outside is beyond our control, unaware that what shows up outside is largely a reflection of what is going on inside. We can end up wandering through our entire time on earth in a sort of confused fog, our lives resembling the voyage of a fallen log in a large lake, living a path sketched out by whatever hits us in the water then arriving at the end of our life's stream only to realize that we failed to live full out.

In the 1980's as a little girl I remember hearing Cyndi Lauper's hit song "Girls Just Wanna Have Fun." The very first time this song hit my ears, it was automatically one of my favorites. The song had an energy that was positively contagious. My aunt, who was a teenager at the time, would dance around the house with her hair-brush microphone like Cyndi in the video. Never one to be left out of a party, I would grab the back of her shirt and dance through the house with her. Looking back, the scene of us skipping through the house screaming lyrics (several made up) is hilarious.

There were a couple of lines that I remember to this day however: "Some boys take a beautiful girl, and hide her away from the rest of the world. I wanna be the one to walk in the sun." Walking in the sun, for me, symbolized fun, freedom, and the confidence to be you no matter what anyone thinks. The "boys" were the people in the world that want to stop you from being you. These lyrics were the inspiration for the title of the book. Cyndi says she wants to walk in the sun, but the song makes me want to dance just like Cyndi.

There is so much freedom in childhood – there is nothing off limits. You think that if you really wanted to fly, you could. Sadly, for most of us, it is here that your beliefs in your own capabilities start being chiseled away. Through physical examples and stories, your brain is constantly bombarded with limitations. Later, when you are an adult, these limitations surface in the form of your everyday life.

What you believe is actually possible for you to achieve. Often we walk through our lives in a sort of daydream, never realizing that the way we see our world is creating the world we see. Most people are on a merry-go-round called "The Same." You think the same thoughts, perform the same activities, entertain the same feelings, BUT desperately want something better to jump on the ride with you. It's never going to happen; you must face yourself in the mirror and decide from this day forward that you are going to live life fully awake and on purpose.

Years back, I ran into a solid brick wall face-first with no hint of cushion, an event where you feel an unexpected BAM! right to the face, nothing, and then you are out faster than a blown out light bulb. When you do regain consciousness, there is confusion as to what happened. In reality, my brick wall was simply a glimpse of what I deep down believed was the truth, a truth that frankly scared me to death, because I understood clearly the implications of that truth.

So when I read it, I became really upset and attacked the issue endlessly for a month without stopping, talking to whoever would give me (or pretend to give me) their ear. For some reason I just felt unable to let the topic go, until my mother said something to me. She raised her head from making her coffee and nonchalantly asked, "Monique, why do you care what anyone writes? Somebody writing a book article or whatever doesn't make it true, and you know that. So why are you going on about what you read like it's the gospel?"

I didn't think it was the gospel, but I did believe what I read. We have all heard at least once, "You only get mad at the truth." Well, I think you actually get angry at what you believe to be the truth. It's our beliefs that create our truths. So, when our beliefs fail to serve us, these untruths hold us back from becoming our greatest selves. When your "truth" gets shaken, either because something disagrees with you, or agrees with you but you wish it did not, there is bound to be an eruption of strong feelings against the offender.

In my case, the offender was research about happiness. The article stated that we have a "happiness maximum." Each of us has a particular level of happiness, regardless of what happens in our life, good and bad. You could win 100 million dollars in the lottery, and if you are an unhappy person, the money might help for a minute, but it won't buy you any happiness.

The reason, supposedly, is that happiness is a matter of genetics. Let's just say, coming from a family background of alcoholism and drug abuse left me less than enthused about my own ability to be happy or for my life to be joy-filled. If you haven't guessed it yet, no matter how much I attacked the research, I wholeheartedly believed what I read. It was impossible for me to recall a time where I had been more than content. On the other hand, it was quite easy for me to recall times that I had been less than content. So there I was, with an article telling me, right to my face, that there was never going to be more.

As a teenager, I thought that once I was able to accomplish some of my goals, my level of happiness or joy would grow up with me. Instead, I found that the events in my life had little to do with the way I felt. Because even when things were going great, I was never more than content. I seem to have had a joy ceiling, and this article was confirming my beliefs. This came at a time in my life when I was feeling stuck, and (yes, that's right) less than content.

I thought to myself: "Just my luck, to read an article like this when I am already feeling badly." The article, however, turned out to be exactly what the doctor ordered. It awakened me from an everyday unconscious place. See, I had been letting life live me – instead of me living life. To be clear, I was not living life on purpose. Sure, I had done some outside work on myself, finished school, gotten married. But there was no search for my true passion, no decision to be joy-filled. My thinking was, "If I do this, I will get that." Each time I felt a downward tilt in my emotions, I asked myself questions like, "What should I do?" instead of "What do I feel in my heart?" or "What do I feel called to do with my life? What will make me make me joyful in my life?"

Instead of a conscious decision to be joy-filled in my life, I was looking outside for answers that could only be answered on the inside. This article, coupled with what was a difficult period in my life, led me to do something I had never done: take a hard look at how I was living, and take responsibility for my living experience. This means working to change a lot of habits, beliefs, and conditioning that have been with me my entire life, keeping what's great, and releasing the less than great. This hard look at oneself is necessary for all those who decide to go from where they are to who they were meant to be. And it's necessary to never stop looking so that you are forever on the path to continuous growth.

I hope that something in this book stirs at least one person to take action in their life right now, to realize that what you get in this one life is determined by your mindset. It has nothing to do with who you are or where you came from. It has everything to do with your self image, how YOU think of you. You will never be any happier than you deeply believe you can be. You will never be any more successful than you believe yourself to be. You have the power to create beliefs that will empower you to get everything you want out of life.

Life has no favorites – your deepest beliefs about yourself will show up in your life every time. If you believe yourself to be powerless and lost, you will find justifications to prove yourself correct. You will connect with those that feel as you do, which reinforces your beliefs. You will unknowingly create experiences in your life that add to this feeling. The opposite is completely true as well. If you feel positive about your life and where your life is going, you will connect with like-minded people. These individuals will be naturally driven and successful with an overall positive outlook on life. You will see a world full of enormous possibilities of what you can accomplish.

We all get handed a mixed bag of great (and less than great) in this life. You are going to find both treats and tricks. The decision, however, on how what you find in the bag shapes your life is up to you. Some bags are going to have more treats than tricks, and others more tricks than treats. You have little control over what goes into your bag in the beginning. You do have control over what you put in your bag later. Yes, life will still throw in her tricks even when it is your turn to add to the bag, but what you do with those tricks is up to you. The best part is that you get to throw in as many treats as you want. It is your thoughts and attitude that will ultimately determine the quality of your bag.

How It All Started

One extremely chilly February morning, a young woman sits in a drug store with her mother waiting to see a doctor. She had been feeling lethargic and losing weight rapidly, having suffered with lung illnesses all of her then short life, she was understandably concerned. Her equally nervous mother sat next to her wondering what it could be this time. The physician looked her over, ran a few tests, and had a diagnosis.

The nurse motioned to Maria, my mother, to reenter the examination room. My mother was perfectly healthy – for a woman one month pregnant. I am told my grandmother became hysterical at the news, and had to be escorted out of the doctor's office. She was shocked, which is a little funny since my mother had been living with a man for a few months by this time.

Eight months later, and three months after her eighteenth birth, Maria gave birth to a caramel-colored baby girl. Although certainly not the last, she was the first person to have a child out of wedlock in our family. This was a big deal considering Maria had been told for years she was premature, because her birthday and her mother's wedding date didn't match.

My family needed the comfort of a pretty lie, because they had no idea that past truths have no power over the great potential of the present. We are not held prisoner by the choices we made. It is the choices we make that are important....because you can't do anything about yesterday. But you can do everything about today, and create a new result. We can continuously redefine the path of our lives by the choices we make in the present.

From the moment we are born, the shaping of our deepest values and beliefs are being quietly formed. Every word we hear and all the actions we witness contribute to who we become. Our memories act as a handbook that we use to explain, or navigate us through the endless twists and turns of life. The problem is that there is usually no objective party to check the accuracy of our handbooks. There is also no one to update outdated or imprecise information. Without a commitment to self-development, you will live a life limited by your memories, and forfeit one that can be lived out of your infinite possibility. Stephen Covey writes, "Through our imagination, we can visualize the uncreated worlds of potential that lie within us."

Like millions, my family shaped how I would later see the world: for the good and the not so much. They were doing their best with the level of awareness they possessed. In short, they did what they knew to do. The quality of my life elevated when I realized you could increase what you know, like the way personal experiences can shape your thoughts. This is important because thoughts lead to actions, and our actions create the lives we live.

The key is to become aware, or conscious, of how our thoughts are causing what shows up in our lives. You can only change what you can see. The easiest way I have found to do this is holding up your results in each area of your life. Ask yourself simply: "Is what I am getting what I want?" Keep what is serving you, and do something new in the areas that aren't. You can do this whether it's family, employment, education, or overall living day to day. Just do not imprison yourself in a mental jail of your own making. Make a decision to direct your thoughts, instead of allowing your thoughts to direct you.

~ CHAPTER 1 ~
How We Get Shaped
(The Women in My Life)

My Grandmother

My grandmother's eyes were not big enough for me once I entered the world. She had not been happy at first about her unwed teenage daughter having a baby. My grandmother had urged her daughter in the months preceding my arrival into this world to terminate the pregnancy, and start clean. She had been less than enthused about the initial announcement of my imminent arrival. But trust me when I tell you, the love and pride that she displayed toward me left no evidence of these previous feelings. "Lil Flo," as she was called by family and friends, was a firecracker to say the least. She said just what was on her mind at the time, and offered no apologies for how you perceived her.

She was the only child my great-grandmother had given birth to. Her birth had been something of a little miracle. Doctors had told my great-grandmother that she could never carry children because of a physical condition. Granma had no idea that she was pregnant; doctors told her that she had a growth in her abdomen, i.e. a tumor. When she started having severe cramping she rushed to the hospital thinking the tumor had ruptured. She went into the hospital praying to God for her life, and woke up thanking God for her baby. And I'm told she was so small (because she was born premature) that her uncles could place her in their coat pockets. Now, this was may be an exaggeration....I have no idea how big jacket pockets were back in 1942.

"Lil Flo" was spoiled by her daddy and provided discipline by her mother. At sixteen, she became pregnant and married a man she would later find out was a criminal. Lil Flo admitted to wanting to become a "woman" to enjoy what she viewed as privileges. One of the privileges was being allowed to sit with the adults rather than being sent in the house with the children. She married a man that would beat and abuse her until the day she saw him being arrested on television for robbing a bank.

It was around this time that she began drinking heavily on a regular basis. This habit would lead her to an early grave at the age of forty-five. Shortly after her first husband went to jail, she met the man I would know to be my grandfather and was the only daddy I ever knew. He was the first man in my life that I believed really loved me, and the only man I ever called daddy.

Lil Flo never let any grass grow under her feet, as the old cliché goes. The moment her first husband was clearly out of her life, she found my grandfather in what we New Orleanians call the country: a marshy area south of the city where the main attraction is the neighborhood bar. She married him, and he adopted my mother and her younger sister. My Aunt Mona was two, and my mother four, at the time of their marriage. My grandmother being a "tell it to your face" person took the divorce papers to the penitentiary for her ex-husband to sign. She could have gotten a divorce without going to the prison, but wanted to show him respect.

My Great-Grandmother

Great-Grandmother, or Granma as I referred to her, had a quiet, loving spirit. But it would be foolish to attempt to take advantage of her, because she had a presence that would knock you down. You knew she meant business when she started speaking Creole. She would often place one finger to her mouth while simultaneously looking at me, and say, "Petit la bouche." I believe these words to mean "small mouth." Yes, I was quite a talker in those days and not too much has changed. But trust me when I say, I knew to be quiet whenever she said it and looked at me.

Granma was born in 1904, the oldest of twenty-four children, and would become mother to the five youngest before the age of thirty. She had watched four of her siblings die in childhood accidents, and buried both of her parents a couple of years apart.

She had grown up in a strict household, where children did what they were told and spoke when spoken to. She once told me that she had been changing diapers and cleaning ever since she could remember being on this earth. Granma had married a man she had no interest in at the age of sixteen to escape her father's constant beatings. She would always say, "I loved my daddy but believe me when I tell you, the Lord knows he was a mean man."

Once, while visiting her mother, her father came in (angry, as usual) and punched her in the face. The hit actually broke her nose. He believed she had said something "sassy," which in the south means disrespectful. He didn't care that she was a married woman of twenty.

Granma had been working since her daddy had taken her out of the first grade. There was no mandatory minimum age to work during her childhood, and even if there would have been, I think that, from the description of her daddy, he would have found a way around it. I fondly think of "Granma" as sort of superhero because of the many struggles she endured. She was sick with various illnesses from the day she was born. According to her mother, her daddy would come into the house, look at her as an infant, and tell his wife, "That baby gonna die." She had more than a few major surgeries and still took care of anyone that ever knocked at her door. Yet, with all the hardships that she had endured she never complained one bit.

She was deeply spiritual and always praised God for the blessings in her life. Granma would talk at length about how she had enjoyed her life. She taught me to tell time, play ring around the rosy, and how to sew a button on a shirt. Granma would sit on the phone with me for hours just listening to my six-year-old ramblings. She made you feel as if every word that came out of your mouth was poetry, constantly commenting on how creative my ideas were, and asking lots of questions.

Granma did this even after her daughter Lil Flo died suddenly six months after her forty-fifth birthday. I would cry for hours over my own ten-year-old heartbreak on the phone to her. As always, she would listen and offer encouraging words. Even while her heart was broken because she had lost her only child, she would often whisper in my ear that she loved me best because I was her eldest great-grand child. Later, she would tell my cousin that he was her favorite because he was the first boy. Granma wanted each of us to feel that we were special because she loved all of her family very deeply. Her house was open to both family and those that might as well have been family.

My Mother

Mama is the eldest of my grandmother's four surviving children. My grandmother gave birth to six children, though her set of twins died as infants: the first was stillborn, and the other passed away at three months old. I remember my grandmother sitting at the kitchen many nights talking about her second baby girl, Debra. Debra was born soon after my mom and before my Aunt Mona.

Lil Flo would sit in the kitchen with her cold glass of Budweiser, staring off and usually talking about a subject totally unrelated, and then (as if a light switch had been lifted) she would tell you how old Debra would have been. She had been born in July, the same as my mother and aunt. Grandmother would describe her daughter as if she had seen her yesterday. She would talk about her full head of beautiful dark hair, her deeply tanned skin, and how pretty an infant she had been.

Two minutes later, as if the light switch had been pushed down again, she would begin another story. This time she would talk about something she had done that was fun. Her happy stories were musicals minus a stage, because she would sing and even dance in her reenactment of whatever story she was telling at the time. Some of these stories originally had no musical numbers in them, but Lil Flo used her creative license to add them. But this perfectly describes my family experience and thousands of others: a bag of happy and sad, up and down, so well-mixed together at times it was hard to discern exactly which cycle you were experiencing.

The vivid account of Debra's death was nothing new to my mother, since she had heard this story and others her entire life. Being the oldest provided the unfortunate privilege of always knowing what was going on with those surrounding her. This is an intense burden to any child, being exposed to the problems of adults when they are not yet equipped to handle the knowing.

Children see the world through a reflection of themselves. They believe themselves involved in what happens in the world around them. This is why children may feel responsible if their parents divorce. They sincerely believe that somehow they caused their parents' decision to separate. Kids that are exposed to large amounts of negativity can end up carrying around misplaced blame and guilt. Left unchecked, they can take these emotions into adulthood – ultimately impacting the quality of their lives. Even if the adults are no longer present, they will continue the pattern of blame and guilt with themselves. We must make the decision to expose our children to exactly what we want them to soak up, because they are sponges. They will soak up whatever is there, so we must only spill the sweetest punch.

My mother Maria has an interest in learning whatever is around her. She will watch something until she understands how to do it. From her, I absorbed the thought that I can learn to do most things. She would say frequently, when I asked her to teach me to cook, "Watch me, do what I do, and that will be all the teaching you need." She's a visual thinker naturally, though this turned out to be a blessing and a curse while growing up. She was blessed because she was extremely independent as a young child. She was cursed because the more she learned what to do, the more she was required to do. My grandmother, who always kept an immaculately clean house, turned over the reins to mama the moment she was capable. By the time mama was twelve, she was cooking, cleaning, and maintaining a house of six. She also acted as director of my grandmother's special projects, such as watching the neighbors' kids. My mother had grown lady responsibilities without being a grown lady.

From the women and other adults in my life I absorbed a variety of qualities. Some that served me well in my life, like the ability to deal with what life throws at you. And what happens to you is what happens – it's your attitude that leads to happiness or sadness. These women made me feel special, like a gift from God they were blessed to receive.

My grandmother would tell me how I was a "Moliere" as if the name entitled me to a place in the royal family. She did this, not out of arrogance or superiority, but because I had no daddy to claim me. She gave me more love before I realized I had less, and therefore I never experienced the difference. My mother has given me more love and support throughout my life than I could have ever imagined. She was the first person to give me a glimpse of looking beyond self-created limits for my life. Every time I ever said I couldn't do something she would ask me, "Why not?" instead of agreeing that my ideas were far-fetched, like others around me. Yes, we have our ups and downs, disagreements, and no agreements. One thing I've never questioned is her dedication to me. These gifts have provided me a life vest for the times that I became disconnected from my life's path.

The Other Side of the Coin

Now, for the other side of the coin: I come from a family where the booze poured like water. One of my aunts was getting drunk most days of the week by the time she was sixteen. Another was dead, because of alcohol, by the time she was thirty-two. Drinking at a young age was the norm back then, because no one realized the tremendous harm it was doing. Everyone was just doing what they had seen done by the adults before them. Thus, the cycle would continue and seemed to worsen with each new generation.

You, of course, got the negative runoff that comes with substance abuse. Those that enable the drinkers end up feeling cheated and trapped by life. There were verbal altercations that often escalated into physical altercations no matter the subject. Finally, there is the cloud of depression that hangs over the heads of everyone directly connected to the abusers. These experiences lead me to be pessimistic about how much happiness one can expect in life. I used the phrase "I'm just being realistic" to uphold generalized negativity about the world.

In truth, there is usually two ways to look at much of what occurs in our lives. Take, for example, the unexpected loss of a job. You could look at it as the worst thing in the world that could have happened to you, and decide to fall directly into a "Why me?" state of mind, and simply spiral downward from there. OR you could look at it as a transition into something else, somewhere else, and into what you were meant to do.

Things Happen

March 31, 1987 was a cold (for springtime) Tuesday morning. Jared, my newest baby brother was four months old. I awakened at six, a full hour before I needed to get up, because of the noise. The baby and my three-year-old brothers were lying in a bed across from me, still sleeping. I remember admiring how cute they looked as I tippy-toed to the bathroom. On my way, I looked into my grandmother's bedroom. My mother and grandfather were talking while attempting to get my grandmother dressed. She was half on the bed, half off, mumbling incoherently. I ran back to my bed down the hall.

My grandmother would have seizures from time to time as a result of her hepatitis. She contracted the disease through a blood transfusion given to her during a surgery. The condition was made worse by her refusal to stop drinking. So, she getting sick and even going to the hospital was nothing new. This day was different somehow. The fear in the voices coming out of bedrooms felt as if they were piercing my eardrums.

Suddenly, I heard my grandmother make a sort of grunting sound. Daddy hollered, "What is that on the floor?" Mother screamed, and I could hear her talking to 911. I saw her run past my room and exit through the hallway door. Daddy made a sound I had never heard before or since, and sincerely pray to never hear again. He sobbed uncontrollably repeating over and over again, "Florence, please, please don't leave me!" I could hear my mother's voice outside screaming, "No, Jesus, please."

I cannot remember exactly at what point I ran outside to the front yard. I remember standing on the porch and watching the paramedics on the 610 interstate above, as they passed my house in error, and hoping they hurried. They came into my home. I heard them say they had a pulse. My grandmother had been unconscious for a while, and would never open her eyes again.

Mother would not go to the hospital with Grandma this last trip. She had gone with her every other time but this one. Every neighbor for four blocks appeared to be in our house. They saw the ambulance and wanted the scoop first hand. I felt so intruded upon, and wished everyone would just get out. You could hear whispering, people wanting to know the details of what happened. One woman actually said, "Looks like we'll have a new man up for grabs."

One particular neighbor told my mother to stop crying, because "that child" (me) was imitating her. She said, "Children don't know what's going on to be sad." How I wish that were true. Some adults fail to acknowledge that children are real people with real emotions. Children are the most sensitive to the emotional effects of change, as a result of their tunnel vision and their dependence on adults. They see everything as being about them, because of their naturally limited view of the surrounding world.

I can remember being completely focused on how Grandma... could she be here on Monday, and just gone on Tuesday? At ten, I knew there was no return from death, at least in this life. I never considered how her death would impact my entire living situation and subsequently end my relationship with the only father I had ever known.

At some point, (though I really cannot recall exactly when) Aunt Mona arrived. She came in and hugged me, while crying and asking for her sister (my mother). Mama was outside again in the cold, not properly covered, on the verge of hysteria. I didn't understand then why she kept retreating to the outside when her emotions got the best of her. Through my own experiences, I now know when pain seems unbearable, you seek to numb it somehow. We all know cold can be both physically and mentally numbing. You can think of nothing except how cold you are. When experiencing heavy emotional upheaval, however, the technique usually fails to lessen pain. The sting of the cold usually goes unnoticed in these instances. The passing of time, combined with faith in a less painful tomorrow, is the best way to overcome emotional aches.

Aunt Mona had gone outside to talk my mother into coming back into the house. She returned, unsuccessful and still sobbing. The phone rang two and a half hours after my grandmother had been rushed to the hospital. Daddy told my mother that she was gone. My grandmother was only forty-five years old at the time of her death. Although my grandmother had a faint pulse when she left, she had already died. She had no brain waves upon reaching the hospital. Later, my mother would tell me she ran out when her mother stopped gasping for breath and became perfectly still.

Less than two years later, my grandfather, the only man I ever called daddy, walked out of my life forever. One day, he just acted as if I had never existed and went on with his new life. I didn't know then, but I would later struggle to deeply love a man.

Sometimes We're Just Drifting

"There are times you are going to see the truck coming and still can't jump out of the way, because you had no idea it was a choice."

In my senior year of high school, most of my classmates were preparing for life after high school. I was preparing to be a teenage mother. One afternoon, I walked into the house to find my momma holding an envelope and looking rather impatient. She asked, what had taken me so long to get home from school. I looked at her and said, half sarcastically, with my teenage flip mouth, "Mama, it's 3:25, school ends at 3:15. You know I do have to walk three blocks." She told me to stop being smart with her and open the letter. I knew the envelope contained an acceptance, or a "Sorry to inform you, look for somewhere else to go" letter from Xavier University. Trying to stall, I said, "Mama you can read it and tell me what it says." Two of the little babies were screaming at this point. Mother was unsuccessfully attempting to calm them. So, I thought it wise to open the envelope before Mama really became annoyed with me.

I read the first line quietly, "Congratulations!" My mother begin yelling excitedly when I shook my head, Yes. In May, I would be the first in the family to graduate from a real high school. In August, I would be the first to ever attend a university. Still, I only felt somewhat excited about the positive things that were happening. I thought to myself, "You're doing what you want to do. Why am I not happier?" I pretended to be happy in front of my mother.

Back then, I chalked my feelings up to being a teenager. In reality, I was focused on what I was going through instead of what I was going toward. My head was screaming, "How is a poor girl like me going to somebody's college?" Rationally, I knew the thought made absolutely no sense. We're in the United States of America, the original land of immense opportunity, right? But when rent and lights is a struggle every month, it gets hard to believe in the American Dream – especially at eighteen. The thing is, we humans act on what we deep down believe about ourselves. These beliefs create pictures in our heads about our actual possibilities. No matter the truth, you will never get further than the picture in your head. The times you do, the vision of you in your head will pull you right back. You must change the vision in your head before you can create the new vision outside.

Later that same month, I became extremely ill with what I thought was the flu. Every afternoon right after I made it home from school, the sickness would start. My appetite had totally disappeared overnight. I never even considered pregnancy, because I thought morning sickness had to occur in the morning. My migraine headaches became more frequent and it seemed impossible to keep my eyes open for any longer than a few hours. Very concerned, my mother scheduled a doctor's appointment after a week of no improvement.

I took a taxicab, without my mother, to the doctor's office because I didn't feel up to the little ones running around the office. Upon hearing my symptoms, the doctor believed an ulcer to be the culprit. Maybe he would have suspected pregnancy if I had not only told him about the nausea and constant heartburn. Needless to say, I was not the most put together eighteen-year-old girl. He explained to me that they were going to place something down my throat that would provide them with a view of my stomach, I think. It happened some years ago, and I am not absolutely sure exactly what the procedure entailed.

A routine pregnancy test was required before the procedure could be performed. There I sat in a high school uniform twirling a ponytail between my fingers waiting to hear a negative result. The nurse walked into the room, lifted the stick and casually said, "You're pregnant." With a blank stare, I whispered, "The test is wrong." She started saying stuff that had nothing to do with what I wanted to hear: "The test measures a hormone in your blood that is only present when you are pregnant, blah blah blah."

At that moment I wanted to just melt into a puddle on the floor. How could I go home with this unfortunate news? What in the world was I to do with a baby, really? A million thoughts were rushing through my terrified young mind at the time. One of my thoughts was about my mother, how she had sat in a doctor's office eighteen years before. I desperately hoped history would be kind to me, and abandon the notion of repeating itself. Now I know history does not repeat itself because we are the masters of our destiny. History is forced to comply with the choices we make. The truth is, even when good events take place in your life, you can find a way to mess it all up. Your real belief is you aren't worthy for one reason or another. Therefore, your mind will lead you to actions that wipe out the positive events in your life.

The doctor came into the room a few minutes after the nurse had abandoned her quest to convince me. He said in a low gentle tone, "There are options other than giving birth available to you." He wrote down the names of a few physicians, patted my shoulder, and walked out of the room. I had never felt so alone or frightened. The cab ride home seemed unusually short this day, and worst, I still had no idea what to tell my mother. I thought, "Maybe keep the pregnancy to myself for awhile, until I can figure out what to do. Yeah, that's exactly what I will do, and tell her the doctor thinks an ulcer is the cause of my sickness." Sometimes, the plans you make up in your head really need to remain there.

Mother was sitting by the door as I entered the house, waiting to find out what was the root of my illness. Mother asked, "So, what did the doctor tell you?"

"He thinks I may have an ulcer, and is going to run tests to be sure."

"When are you scheduled to go back for the tests?"

"I will call to make an appointment after exams next week."

"Okay, so what did he prescribe for your pain?"

"Nothing, because he has to be sure about the ulcer first." My voice began to rise at this point, because I felt worn out by the continuous questions. She looked at me with a look that said, You better say something that makes sense, girl.

All of a sudden, before I could pull the words back, I said, "The doctor said I'm pregnant, okay, that's why I'm sick, that's why he isn't prescribing anything."

~ CHAPTER 2 ~
The Lives We Live
Are the Sum of Our Choices

I had really hoped to avoid becoming another poor teenage mother. But I had never made the choice to avoid becoming another teenage mother. I was muddling through my young life, allowing things to happen – a situation that is repeated over and over throughout many of our adult lives (the muddling, not teenage pregnancy).

We clearly focus in on what we don't want or like, but we never actively go after what we do truly desire. So we end up with what we focused on the most. The law of attraction states in simplest form that "Like attracts like." There are no distinctions made between "do and don't," there is only "do." For example, "I don't want to become a young mother" becomes "I want to be a young mother." Therefore, we must keep our thoughts clearly centered on what we want in our lives.

The problem is we live in a society that has socialized us to concentrate on the negative. We lead with the negatives in our day, and give the positives an "at least" or "it could have been worst." Are you questioning whether this assessment is true? Here's a simple test: ask several people you know, "How was your day?" Some will say "It was okay," in an almost disappointed voice, which means "Nothing happened that I can complain to you about." Others will answer with "Not good," and their voice will become animated as they run down their lists of mishaps. A select few will say, "I had a great day," and even half of those will tell you what didn't go wrong, instead of everything that went right.

Every moment we are blessed to take a breath, we are creating the lives we experience. Our thoughts are real "things" that we bring into life. We choose the thoughts that we think, and good or bad that is exactly what we attract into our lives. Our thoughts are, however, affected by external and internal stimuli. This is why it is of the utmost importance to be aware of what you are allowing into your mind at all times. The internal stimuli are the result of self-talk, or subconscious ideas, we formulated as far back as childhood. The external stimuli are all the information we take in when communicating with other people, watching the news, or using one of our many technological devices.

Happiness and Goals

Somewhere we learned that the road to fulfillment is paved with endless tasks. We lead disorganized, disgruntled lives wondering why true fulfillment is elusive. Is it a great mystery that studies have found 75% of American doctor's visits are due to a stress-related ailment? Measuring life via completed tasks will provide temporary emotional gratification. Unfortunately, the feeling will be temporary. Long-lasting gratification can only be found through fulfilling goals based on your core values. Right now, many are thinking about their infinite lists to complete. Often, you associate dissatisfaction with your inability to complete various tasks. Cleaning house, going to work, going to class, picking up the kids – these are all necessary activities. The accumulation, however, of "checked-off "duties will not alone create happiness nor personal fulfillment.

Some believe happiness is a tangible object that can be attained through acquiring things, or improved personal circumstances. Yes, lots of people may feel a momentary uplift due to a particular achievement, such as a long awaited promotion to a new position in your company, going back to school to finish your studies, your child making the principle's honor roll, or even getting that new shiny car you having been dreaming of every night. You will ultimately return to an empty place, though, if you are not already happy. The key is to truly become happy with where you are presently standing. Decide to enjoy where you are, right where you are standing. This decision will fill you with joy in the present and build a positive foundation for your future. I know that if you are currently struggling to make ends meet, this may seem (on the surface) impossible. I have had to borrow from Peter to pay Paul more times than I care to recall.

These eight statements have tremendously improved my sense of wellbeing, regardless of what's going on outside:

1. It Is What It Is

The majority of situations that occur in life occur to us all in one form or another. Life is like the financial economy: you have up-cycles and down-cycles throughout the years. Some people's down-cycles last longer because they focus on being down.

Therefore, even when they are up, they believe they are still down. So refuse to spend precious time asking "Why me?" An answer to that question will only pull you deeper into despair anyway. Secondly, why complain? The late Mr. Jim Rohn says, why complain about "Seed, soil, and sunshine." You take what you have been blessed with (seed, soil, and sunshine), and grow something spectacular. Go do more with your piece of earth than you ever imagined possible.

2. The Man with No Feet

There is always someone in the world somewhere with it worse than you. Often, we even know someone directly that is experiencing a greater life challenge than us. Here's an old cliché, "I once complained that I had no shoes. Until I saw a man who had no feet." You always have more than what you think. Many of us are allowing ourselves to be conditioned to see what is wrong in our lives. We give personal prizes of recognition to the daily dilemmas and barely honorable mention to what is great in our lives. Learn to appreciate the countless treasures in your life, and your entire world will open up to more.

3. Mirror Mirror on the Wall

Looking in **the mirror** saying affirmations does work. Those that claim otherwise are usually missing an important element. You must believe the words that are coming out of your mouth. If you are affirming in the mirror that you are going to be a millionaire, and you are doing nothing to bring that into reality, you have my permission to stop affirming….because it's never going to happen. On the other hand, if you are doing the work involved in becoming what you are affirming, your affirmations will both inspire and propel you to bring your goals into reality.

4. Vampires Will Suck You Dry

Here's the skinny: there are people in your life that should be removed. You know exactly who they are without thinking too hard. These are the people that bring no value to your life. They constantly criticize your dreams, and make you regret even opening your mouth to speak. These people must go if you are to grow into who you want to be. These people suck precious positive energy, just like a vampire sucks blood. It takes energy to fight off their negativity, and this is a waste of valuable resources. You will need all the energy you can gather up to improve you. Find those that lift you up with their voice and energy. Also, work to be a valuable friend yourself. That way, you will be able to give quality friendship as well as receive.

5. Lucky is as Lucky Does

My old definition of "lucky" was grand opportunities that appear to come out of nowhere. Now I know the real definition of "lucky" is grand opportunities that appear out of persistent effort taken. The more you do, the luckier you seem to be. You want to be Mr. or Mrs. Lucky? Decide what you want to do and get busy doing it. Good things rarely simply fall out of the sky. What appears to be luck is usually a direct result of consistent action and positive expectations. Incorporate those two into your life and everyone will swear you are one of the "lucky" people.

6. Time is a Gift

The time we are given in this life is a gift from God, whatever form God takes for you personally. We should spend it working on all the things we CAN do, remembering all the people we can love, and all the service we can offer. We can choose not to waste precious time agonizing over unchangeable circumstances.

Worrying does nothing to solve what's worrying you. Spend time engineering solutions to your challenges and then implement those solutions. Whatever has to be, let be.

7. Lights, Camera, Action

We all listen to the little voices in our head nudging us in one direction or another. That's why it's so important for our intentions and goals to be the director of these voices. Usually our fears and past programming are directing the entire show. In these productions, we play the extra in the background – never the star. Our fears end up with the lead role in these made-in-our-brain movies. Shut down these voices with objections: "Others have done what I want to do. I can do it too." At first you may feel a little silly saying this to yourself. I still do. That's just your old habits attempting to pull you back into the fold. Keep turning around the negative self-talk into positive self-talk. Over time, your mind will provide you with more and more empowering voices.

8. Practice Makes Better

Some subscribe to the "fake it till you feel it" mentality. You pretend to be what you want to be. I think if it works for you, great! Because the important point is to find what works. The faking part of the equation doesn't work for me, though, because it seems disingenuous. I like the term practicing. Practicing being someone I intend to be – that works much better for me. I know the more I practice something, the better I will become at doing or being. This creates the belief that I am growing into something new, which is more believable for me. I could pretend the rest of my life, and if I never believe deep down that I can change, nothing much would change.

Bottom line, happiness takes a conscious effort on the part of a lot of us. By default we tilt to the negative side of life. In today's world you never have to look too hard for reasons to feel badly. Look at the news or call one of your friends, not to mention when stuff we never expected to occur does. Loved ones leave the earth, marriages that we believed would last a lifetime fall apart. Life happens when we least expect it, without any apologies for the inconvenience. It can become easy to dwell on what's wrong, and forget all the right that's present in our lives.

Then there are those that claim to be happy, spiritually uplifted, and goal focused. Most of our unconscious daily affirmations, however, point to the opposite: "I hope no one gets in my face today at work" or even, "Today, is not going to be a good day, I can just feel it in my bones."

We walk around with scowls on our faces and negativity in our hearts. Have you ever heard, "A bad tree will yield no good fruit?" Believe me, your thinking is standing between you and your best possible life.

We look externally for what we need to be happy internally. We say things like, "I can be happy when I finish school," "I can be happy when we are married," "I need to purchase my dream home to feel completely satisfied." Fulfillment is an emotion born in our hearts, and not in the things we acquire. Happiness is a state of mind, not a destination on a map.

Happiness First, Goals Second

You must be happy in your own skin right now or any goal you fulfill will leave you saying, "Okay that's it." The mere completion of a task, regardless of difficulty, will never provide overall wellbeing. You simply can't fix an inside problem from the outside. This is why all real personal development is focused on the power of positive thinking. I have spent a number of years in a half-attaining, periodically content mental state attempting to fix externally what has to be dealt with internally.

You have to make the decision to be happy with what you have and where you are right now. Happiness is what allows you to create goals born out of your heart, goals that represent the true person you were supposed to be. Goals that have probably been buried underneath your mental junk. Happiness takes you out of "should do" and "ought to", and moves you directly into "called to." It becomes your energy source when you inevitably hit the bumps in the road that keep you from who you want to be.

Getting more than you presently have requires a serious belief in your own ability to get it. It is impossible to have a strong belief in oneself and still be unhappy. I am not saying there aren't a lot of miserable people out there that gain success in a specific area. We have numerous athletes that are champions on the field, but whose personal lives are a "hot mess," examples that you can be dynamic one place and falling apart at the seams in another. Getting more than you presently have means BECOMING more than you presently are. Truly becoming more is a systemic change that naturally improves your life in other areas.

There was a story in a popular magazine about this woman who now competes in body building competitions. The story began with two pictures of this beautiful lady. In one she was obviously considerably overweight. In the other picture, she strutted a lean muscular physique. You know it was one of those Before and After deals that you see on weight-loss commercials. The picture stopped me, but the story got me. She said that she had once been in good physical shape. Over the years, however, her love of food had outpaced her desire to be fit.

The decision to change came when she ran into someone that hadn't seen her in years. They told her that she was hardly recognizable because of her weight gain. That day, she made the commitment to change her life by reducing her weight. A woman on a mission to succeed, she got friends to participate in her new regiment. Together they changed the way they ate and exercised more. This new energy leads her to look for something new to challenge herself. After losing much of her weight, she wanted to tone her body. She decided to start lifting weight just to gain a little muscle. Her new confidence in what she could accomplish led her to start entering competitions. In the article, she talked about her new energy, confidence, and belief in herself.

That one goal improved the whole person. It was more than a target on a dart board. Her goal even helped those that chose to get involved with her. Her friends lost weight and improved their eating habits to enjoy an enhanced life. She could have gone on a crash diet, or exercised and reduced her calories to lose the extra pounds. Even if she did so unknowingly, she made a decision that led to systemic change. Becoming more was the real destination. Releasing weight merely initiated the journey and the weight loss was a perk. In both pictures she was smiling, and said she very much loved her life of travel and get-togethers with friends. Her decision to release the pounds was not enough to make her happy. Although I'm quite sure it fueled her journey and provided one more notch on her happiness board.

If she had measured happiness by the size of her waist, releasing the weight would have brought her momentary joy. One of three things takes place in this type of scenario: 1) The weight would have returned to her. 2) She would have become obsessed with a particular number on the scale. 3) She would have found something new with which to be dissatisfied. Unhappiness is a bottomless pit that cannot be closed with an external plug. People that focus on a particular goal to make themselves happy end up no better than they began, even when they reach the "finish line." This is why deciding to be happy by appreciating everything that's great in your life is essential. The real goal is to improve you through the change that will take place to accomplish your goal.

~ CHAPTER 3 ~

Happiness Lies Within

Some people search for happiness. You can't find happiness because it's not lost. It is inside of us all hiding under our emotional covers.

My friends and I would frequently joke about "happy people." We made statements like, "You can never trust a person that doesn't frown." All of us ladies, and a few men, agreed there was absolutely nothing to be happy about every day. We bought into the mindset of the "herd" without questioning its validity. The herd is most of the people that we allow to surround us. These individuals largely influence our choices. Our circles are often pessimistic in their views toward living well and completely. The default, outside world influences can be grim, and in that spirit we set out to live our lives. The people with whom we interact provide unconscious reinforcement that keeps us stuck in our current life patterns. We believe those persons that exude inner fulfillment are "a special breed" or merely pretending.

 Everyone in the world has the same opportunity to be "great." Being great means living a happy fulfilled life within your designed purpose. Living within your designed purpose is a choice that the individual makes. I thought for the longest time that I would be forced to exist in a sort of middle space. A life of not really sad and not really happy, essentially just getting through each day "the best I knew how at the time." When asked, "Are you happy?" I would quickly respond with an "I'm content with the way things are right now," which is the equivalent of "No, I'm not ready to do cartwheels in the middle of my living room, but I wouldn't slit my wrist just yet either." In my mind, being content was the most a "regular person" could hope to achieve. In truth, happiness is the divine birthright of all human beings even if we are unable to see it.

Many of us are so locked into our patterns of surviving life that we fail to see this truth. The ups and downs of employment, personal relationships, child rearing, finances, and living can make you feel like the ball in a ping pong game. You are tossed back and forth across the table of life knowing that you are going to get smacked. It can be difficult to believe that consistent happiness is possible when life is continuously changing.

The key is to become the singular constant in your life, regardless of what changes occur around you. In experiments you have a constant and then variables that are tested. A scientist measures the change in results with each new variable. The thinking being, each new variable may create a different result. This strategy works well in scientific experiments. I think the constant and variable application (with some slight modifications) is useful in the pursuit of becoming the "happiest you." What if the results remained unchanged despite the variable? This is exactly what people who are successfully living life practice every day.

An individual has the power to become what I call an "unyielding constant." This is exactly what a person living within their purpose does: they know what is important in their lives and they allow nothing to push them off their chosen course. The landscape along their road may inevitably transform depending on the season, but the vision of their destination is clear. These individuals can be young or old, rich or financially challenged. Their purpose-directed thoughts are the constant in the experiment known as "life."

Many of our routes in life are being dictated by the direction of "life's wind." The wind picks us up and drops us off somewhere. Once placed in a new spot, we begin to make decisions based on where we land. You look around at the current landscape and begin to react, rather than respond, to your new situation. Thoughts based in this theory make a lot of sense on the thin surface. Why take the time to develop a response, if you have no idea where you going to be next?

Becoming an "unyielding constant" provides the ability to plan your life. You create a path that you are going to stick with regardless of the weather. Successful people have "no matter what" goals that guide their decisions in life. They experience unforeseen circumstances just like everyone else does – it is their response to these unforeseen circumstances is what differs.

The beauty of sunshine is available to everyone. Sometimes, we just have to make our own.

Here's a great story of a woman who understood how to be an "unyielding" constant:

Sarah Breedlove, better known as Madame C.J. Walker and the first female African American self-made millionaire, was no stranger to hardship. She was born to ex-slaves on a plantation in the south. Her parents, once freed, worked as sharecroppers. Madame Walker started working with her parents only a few years out of diapers. She was an orphan by the young age of seven due to an outbreak of yellow fever. Shortly after her parents' death, Sarah and her older sister moved across the river to find work.

They both found jobs working as maids for well-off white people. Madame Walker married at only fourteen years of age to escape her sister's abusive husband. Her only daughter was born out of this union three years later. By nineteen years of age, she was already a widow and single mother. She decided to move with her daughter away from the south to St. Louis, Missouri to wash other people's clothes for pay. It was during this period that her life would begin to change forever.

Still Sarah Breedlove, it was in St. Louis she would marry briefly for the second time. Her marriage would ultimately end in divorce, leaving her alone once again. Sarah, always the mover, became a member of St. Paul's African Methodist Episcopal Church. In this church, she met well-educated black people that lead her to become more aware of her appearance.

She was still a young woman, but already losing her hair. Sarah had tried numerous products in an attempt to stop shedding hair with no real results. She then began experimenting with different products being sold at the time. Nothing she tried worked very well for her, and she began concocting her own recipes. Supposedly, a man came to her in a dream one night with the exact ingredients she needed to use to create a hair product that worked to prevent hair loss.

The product worked for her and other ladies that she knew. She believed there was too much competition in St. Louis so Sarah moved to Denver, where her sister in-law lived, to setup her new business. She worked as a cook until she could afford to quit her job. Once Madam Walker left her employment as a cook, she split her time between washing clothes for extra money and pushing her product.

A close friend of hers, a man named C.J. Walker, moved to Denver to be with her. The couple married and that is when Sarah Breedlove became Madam Walker. Her new husband had experience with developing newspaper advertisements. He helped his wife create a mail order business to sell her hair products. Mr. Walker eventually wanted to stop expanding the business, because he felt they were successful enough, but Madam Walker wanted to march forward to enrich not only her life but the lives of other women. The two divorced when they were unable to reach an agreement. She began to hire beauticians and saleswomen to place her products in the hands of more ladies.

Madam Walker, formerly Sarah Breedlove, hired thousands of agents to market her hair products around the country. Madam Walker's employment of women allowed those women to better provide for their families. No one would have blamed her if she had lied down and accepted only what life threw at her. She refused to allow circumstances determine how much success she could expect in life. Regardless of what variables life threw in her way, she continued forward. She became an "unyielding constant" and allowed nothing to derail her one-way train.

Madam Walker was able to achieve her goals in a time when women especially black women were largely viewed as unequal to men. She experienced firsthand struggles that we can't even imagine in this era. Yet, Madam Walker decided what she wanted out of life and went after it until life couldn't refuse her.

~ CHAPTER 4 ~
Attitude Isn't Everything...
It's Just 90% of Everything

Happiness is more than a one-day event it's an everyday commitment that only you can make.

Here's the skinny: there's no special potion that can snap good feelings into you. We are individually responsible for the happiness we enjoy, or don't. Some people seem to wake up on the right side of the bed every morning. I have no idea why some just have a naturally sunny disposition regardless of what's going on in their lives. I guess this is just one more item on the "that's the way it is" chart of life.

I do know that you can consciously choose to be happy. It was Viktor E. Frankl that said, "Everything can be taken from a man but one thing: the last of the human freedoms—to choose one's attitude in any given set of circumstances, to choose one's own way."

Your attitude in this world, in each breath you take, is always a choice. The length of time you have been practicing a particular attitude is meaningless. That's right I said "practice." Because that's what you have been doing – practicing. I do not believe a negative seminal state to be natural for human beings. I believe the universe to be an abundant, continuously creating space. Abundance is produced from positive energy, and I am a creation born out of that space. Therefore, how could any type of sustained negativity be natural? Yes, you will get down at times. Everybody does. It is the STAYING down that can become a habit that leads to a life wasted.

Happiness is an attitude that you decide to commit yourself to. We may not control every event that happens in our lives. We do control our attitudes toward whatever happens. It is unrealistic to think that the good times are going to last forever. It is just as unrealistic to believe that the bad times are going to last forever. What makes the difference, between events causing you to stumble or knocking you face down on the ground, is attitude.

Life's One Certainty

The one certainty we have on this wonderful journey of ours is change. There is not one single thing that stays the same. So, why do we fight against change? We fight change out of the fear of what comes next. We fear making the wrong decisions. We fear failing at what we choose to do. We fear regretting decisions. We fear the opinions of friends and family. Our fears and uncertainties block us from living productive purpose-filled lives.

Much of what we fear will either never happen or will happen no matter how much we fear. Therefore the decision to live in fear as a daily practice is, quite frankly, pointless. Now don't get me wrong, a little healthy fear in some areas is good. If man was totally fearless, we might no longer exist. A little fear encourages you to wear a seatbelt when you drive, or look both ways before you decide to step out into traffic. It stops you from jumping off cliffs (or to at least have a bungee cord connected to your body when you do).

The crazy part of the whole situation is that anything meaningful in our lives only takes place when change occurs. We marry and bring children into the world: change. We move to a new city for better career opportunities: change. You enter life a baby, grow into a child, and ultimately become an adult: big change. Even if you stood in one spot, change is still occurring. In reality, it is impossible to stand still because the entire earth is moving in space. Acting when change happens is adaptation, and everything in nature adapts or dies. Human beings are not excluded from this reality. The primitive animal has a great advantage over us. He follows and accepts change more readily than human beings. If his food supply dries up, he searches for a new supply. Some of us would sit around hoping the food returned like magic, and when it did not, we would simply wither away and ultimately die. The ability to adapt is only useful when we use it proactively to respond to change.

The only security in life is the perspective that, no matter what happens, you will more than survive. You will take something from the experience, and use it to thrive.

Life can change in a blink of an eye.

During my college years, my mother worked as a night desk clerk/housekeeper at a motel near our home for a while. It was the kind of place where ten-dollar prostitutes brought their "tricks," and the "tricks" asked for change. Drug use was so common in the establishment, the owner actually provided tools for her patrons to do drugs. According to her, "They are going to smoke anyway, and I don't want them tearing up my shXX!"

Yeah, that makes sense in a bizarre world where the entire universe is turned inside out. You know, where down becomes the new up and up becomes the new down. This would not have been anyone's dream job with immense growth possibilities. The job did provide late hours that meant she could see the little ones off to school and, being a stone's throw from our house, it had a cheap commute.

Most days, Mama's shift ended around six in the morning. Sometimes she would stay and talk to the lady who took over after her. She might also be a little late if the night happened to be particularly busy and she needed to finish a few rooms. So, I would never be very concerned if she wasn't home immediately after work.

I happened to be awake this particular Sunday morning because of final exams. I had been redoing accounting problems all night. Procrastination always led to entire night cram sessions right before big tests. At about 6:30 am, my teenage brother started moving around the small apartment in expectation of our mother walking through the door. At 7:30, my mother had still not come home and I began to feel very uneasy.

It's strange…somehow you often know when something has happened to a loved one without being told. You can just feel it deep inside of you when a terrible event has taken place. My brother came in and said, "I'm going check on Mama, she should have been home by now." At this point, I could no longer pretend to be studying. What had begun as a small feeling of uneasiness had grown into the full-blown knowledge that something bad had happened. Now I was sitting in my bed praying that Mama just wasn't dead. I spoke to God, "Lord I can deal with anything except her being dead."

A little while later, my brother ran into the house screaming, "Mama was rushed to the emergency room in an ambulance." I threw on jeans and a shirt from the night prior, asked one neighbor to watch the still sleeping children, and my brother had already asked another neighbor to drop us both off at the hospital. Once at the hospital, we could not get any information on our mother's condition until the fifteen minute visiting time. The worst part was that visiting hours were every two hours and unfortunately we had just missed one. No doctor or even a nurse would tell us anything until the visiting hour. The owner of the motel told my brother that she had been attacked in a robbery. He had no other details about the incident. I sat there with my brother endlessly throwing out worst-case scenarios: What if Mama dies? What if Mama has brain damage? What will happen to my seven siblings if Mama doesn't come home? What if, what if, what if! The "ifs" in life will drive you crazy if you let them.

Twenty minutes after first arriving at the hospital I was having a full-blown panic attack. I was well acquainted with the signs. At ten, the day after my Grandmother's funeral, I was standing in the kitchen alone and my chest began to tighten, I struggled to breathe, and felt dizzy. The attack lasted, in real time, just a few minutes, but in my mind it felt like hours. Later, when my mother took me to the doctor he announced with a smile, "Congratulations, you had your first panic attack." I'm guessing it was his attempt at light humor or something.

Today, I knew emotionally taking myself out the game was not an option because, without Mama, I was the only adult. There were no daddies or extended family to call upon for help, just me and seven children.

My brother was driving me crazy in the hospital with his endless chatter. He was saying his worst-case scenarios out loud, because he was really scared too. I would have strangled my brother that day and then broken into a million pieces on the floor, but there were some sentences I said to myself that stopped me. No, I had not yet made a commitment to become a student of lifelong personal development. No, there was no affirmation that I recited then and there to turn me around in an instant. I simply used what was already inside me, because I believed there to be no other choice in the situation. I told myself what happens is what happens, and now I have to deal with it – there's nothing else to do.

We are all naturally creative, resourceful, and whole. There is nothing about us that needs to be fixed. We simply need to become aware of our strengths so that like any great tool, they are available to us on demand. I pulled these skills unconsciously out of myself because I needed to survive the moment. Little did I know then, these skills could be used to thrive instead of survive. The skills we need to move forward in any area of our lives are already within us. We just have trouble accessing them on demand because we live unconsciously, for the most part. Think about it. If you have decided that you are afraid of failing, that's a decision. It is not a state based in fact. If you were asked to think of instances that you had to show courage, you could think of times in your life where you had been brave. Therefore, you have the ability to be courageous. For whatever reason (beliefs, habits, or past conditioning), you aren't utilizing the skill.

Some of us only pray or seek God's council in extremely stressful moments. Our commitment to prayer is directly tied to the depth of our personal difficulties at the time. Sadly, many of us never realize prayer and connection to our higher power can do so much more than help you survive a particular moment. These practices will actually improve the quality of your life, if used regularly, and the more you use the techniques, the more benefits you will derive. Whatever you wholeheartedly practice consistently, you inevitably become. Practice being calm and you will, without a doubt, become a calm person. Every day of our lives we practice our beliefs in regards to who we are. The person you wake up as is a combination of only two components: decision and dedication.

My mother, through God's grace, more than survived. She thrived, making a full recovery. She had been beaten to the point of concussion. It would take her a while to fully recover from the attack, but she did.

The Way We See the World

Simply stated, the decisions we make determine the lives we live. Our decisions are largely attributed to our belief structure. We all see the world through our own eyes, literally. You also see the world through your beliefs. You then make life decisions based on exactly what you see. The only problem is that you are looking at the world through cloudy glasses. Human beings process new information with comparisons to the old. Unless you make a consistent effort to change your negative belief structures, you will be forever imprisoned by self-limiting assumptions.

Aside from the twelve years spent living with my grandparents, most of my life has been spent living in the "hood." I came of age in New Orleans during the mid-nineties, when we first became the "murder capital of the nation," the rampant police corruption era. On any given night you could be awakened by gunfire. Hours later you would be greeted by police crime scene tape in the morning. Oh, let's not forget a complete repeat of the entire scenario the next day. At least once a month for a year there was somebody I had gone to school with that was in the obituaries. I thought of my teen years as being the beginning of life, but sadly for some of my classmates it was the end. These are the type of experiences that can leave a lasting impression on the way in which you view the world.

Presently, we reside in a working middle-class neighborhood in the southern region of the country. The homes are largely well kept, neighbors wave good morning hellos, and criminal activity is relatively low. Yet, old "thinking" or "belief structures" can be hard to leave behind. The main reason is because they provide a way for us to understand our environment.

I have to read the newspaper every day of the year. There is just no way around this almost compulsive need. My primary goal is to find out what's going on around town. It's important for me to skip the negative articles, to keep my mind positive. The first thing I do after moving to a new place is to find the nearest place to purchase a daily newspaper. This time, my husband suggested having the paper delivered upon moving into our house, since he is usually the one to go out and purchase the paper. Reluctantly I agreed and began home delivery. The very first day the paper should have arrived, there was no paper in sight. The customer service representative assured me the paper would be delivered the following morning. My first thought? Someone has stolen my newspaper right off the front lawn. Why did I jump to this idea? In my neighborhood, there was no such nonsense as having a paper delivered. We had to physically go to the store and purchase newspapers because they would get stolen right off your doorstep.

The address had changed. Parts of my thinking, however, had obviously remained the same. Even when you work on yourself constantly, old programming (i.e. beliefs and conditioning) will still arise. Coming from a place where there was not a lot of abundance can create a scarcity mentality, which is when you believe, often unconsciously, that there just isn't enough to go around in the world. Many of us have this belief, even those that didn't grow up in the "hood." You may believe there aren't enough well-paying jobs. You may believe there aren't enough good men in the world. You feel envious when others find success because you feel it's taking away from your "piece of the pie." You may believe it is necessary to quickly take advantage of an opportunity before it's gone.

One should make decisions quickly, not foolishly. Putting money into investments you don't know much about because your ship might sail is a great example. It was Wallace D. Wattles that wrote in *The Science of Getting Rich*, "You are to become a creator, not a competitor; you are going to get what you want, but in such a way that when you get it every other man will have more than he has now." Whatever you want in this world is there for you. It's our habits and beliefs that tell us otherwise.

Have you ever heard, "Money doesn't grow on trees?" I am sure you have, and like me you may have said it yourself a few hundred times. I was in a retail store once when I heard a little girl about the age of four ask her mother for a shirt. The mother opened her purse and said, "Let me see if I have any money left."

The little girl, sitting next to her mother's purse in the cart, dove her head in behind her mother's hands. She asked her mother, "Do you have anything left?"

Statements like these continue to train our minds (and the minds of the next generation) to believe that there isn't enough. No, I'm not telling you to go out and spend recklessly because that's not abundance. Abundance is a state of being that allows you to feel full and without worry. Spending money recklessly creates worry and implies scarcity. How about saying instead, "It's not a financial priority right now." Or a personal favorite, "I choose to use my resources elsewhere." This places the power back in your hand, because you are making the choice not to purchase the item.

Now I know what you are thinking. That's fine if it's a three dollar box of Cracker Jacks. But what about that new $80,000 Mercedes Benz I have been seeing in my dreams? That might not be a priority, but I want it and can't get it with the coins in my pocket. First, I would suggest you start getting a clear picture of what you claim you want. You may want the $80,000 car because you believe it isn't possible for you to get it, which is scarcity again. So you choose what you believe you can't have to prove your negative belief once more. A person can't have everything they want in this life. Get clear first on whether or not you truly want what you say you want. I have seen vision boards with lavish houses and celebrities pinned on them. The owners of some of these boards work minimum-wage jobs with no plans to increase their incomes.

I'm a positive thinker, but that car probably isn't going to show up on your doorstep any time soon. Start concentrating on the feelings you will feel once you are in possession of that $80,000 dollar car. Think about the smell of the leather when you open the door. If it's a convertible, imagine the wind blowing through your hair. This is your visualization, so it needs to be whatever feels real for you. This exercise will fill you up before you ever step into that brand-new car. It's never the thing or the money we are wanting – we want the feeling that comes with having what we want. Therefore, if you create the feeling you want before having, you can begin playing with the toys before they show up under the tree. You may also uncover what you are really after. Lasting, positive results will never be sustained without inward change. Your personal view (if flawed) will impede positive growth. Many have escaped the entrapments of their environments only to find a second trap: their own belief structure.

~ CHAPTER 5 ~
Quantity vs. Quality of Life

My Mama once told me, "God smiles each time a girl is born into the world, because women are the nurturers of the earth baby." Mother must have repeated this statement a million times in the course of my growing up. To be honest, I never really understood what she meant. The depth of her smile was my only clue that it was something good.

On my thirteenth birthday, when she repeated the phrase for the one-millionth time I asked, "How do women nurture the earth?"

She looked at me, obviously a little surprised at the question, and said, "You can only nurture what you love, and a woman's love is unmatched." Sounds good, but I still had no idea what she was telling me. That knowledge would come much later.

Little girls begin practicing their nurturing skills immediately. Have you ever watched a four year old with her favorite doll? Little Debbie (the doll) will be held from sun up to sun down, during play time, dinner time, bath time, and of course bedtime. Boys are given trucks they can push or balls they can throw. A doll on the other hand is a pretend person that we must take care of. Let me be clear: I am not advocating the end of giving baby dolls to girls. I loved my dolls and enjoy playing dollies with my daughter probably more than I should. The example is only to show the difference between males and females.

Frankly, there is nothing better than being a female. The ability to buy clothes has to be near the top of the list of reasons to be a woman. A man buys a shirt, tie, maybe a jacket depending on the occasion, and he is done. Yeah, if he possesses a smidgen of taste he will look better than his male counterparts. Still, he is no match for a stylish, well-put-together woman. We are a work of art from the tops of our heads to the bottom of our feet. Entire magazines and television shows are devoted to the fashions of women. We have not even begun to discuss jewelry or how the mere height of a female shoe can weaken a man's knees.

Many girls fall in love with clothes, shoes, jewelry, and makeup in the womb. I lie to you not, my barely two-year-old daughter is already picking out her daily outfits. Yes, every stitch that lies against her soft skin is an outfit. Her socks must match the color of her night gown otherwise you will hear a screech of, "Not the same Mama." Doesn't she sound like a doll? Boys are completely opposite. Iron a pair of pants, a shirt, and they are good to go. Sometimes I wonder if all of these perks are to soften the twists and turns we face in life.

Today, a little girl can grow up to become just about anything her heart desires. She can be a CEO of a major company or a heart Surgeon. She may want to become a beautician, a make-up artist, or a nurse. Little Tanya can even work in construction and build skyscrapers side by side with men. Today, more women are not only graduating from college, we are graduating in larger numbers than our brothers. Yes, the last fifty years have been very good to us. So, why are many of us not more fulfilled? What's missing in our lives?

Remember, I began with women from birth are nurturers, and by proxy, emotional creatures. You cannot be nurturing and unemotional at the same time. Herein lies the problem: we want to be everything to everyone and rule the world with an iron fist draped in a pink glove. We still want to be ladies, after all.

Our list of womanly duties has grown these fifty years, regardless of where we are in our lives or what type of lives we choose. The professional mother must balance work, kids, possibly a husband, and attempt to have a social life. The stay-at-home mom must balance work (at-home-moms work too), kids, a husband, and attempt to have a social life. The young college graduate must balance work, possibly a child, a husband (or the pursuit of one), and attempt to have a social life. We must constantly attempt to achieve our goals while standing as caretakers to the world. Whew, is it really hard to imagine that our happiness would inevitably take a back seat?

Are you Handling Business or Busyness? Hamsters on a Wheel

Many of us are falling short in strengthening our quality of life because the wrong scales are being used. Success is often measured by the number of activities we perform in a given day. Did we pick the children up from karate training? Did we pick up the dry cleaning? Is tonight's dinner prepared? Did we email thus and so? Are we volunteering for enough projects?

We walk around with little devices in our ears to prove we are too busy to hold a phone. There are numerous devices to count, record, and categorize human functions. There are calendars integrated into cell phones. Online friend sites provide the opportunity to keep friends abreast of our every move, if we choose. We can talk on the phone, email, instant message, and watch television all at once. We involve ourselves in countless activities, some important and others not so much.

We brag to everyone who will listen just how busy we are. I know people who describe, with their chests poked out, their busyness. Being completely overwhelmed has become the new status symbol in our society. I ask friends how they are doing, and nine out of ten times they will say, "Busy."

I overheard two ladies in the supermarket talking. One said "Enjoying your day off?" Her friend responded, "Well, it's not really a day off because I have a million things to do." She sounded extremely defensive about having a day off! More activities than you can comfortably handle is not a grand achievement because you are losing something valuable in the melee you call your life. You are depriving yourself of the opportunity to carve out the life that you truly desire: a life created out of what you, and you alone, value most.

It is important to notice that I stipulate a value-centered life. Alternatively, you can call it creating the life of your dreams. Often, if you ask someone to describe their dream life, they will start telling you how she would love to have enough money to never have to work again. You would hear a description of their 10,000 square feet customized mansion in Maui, the trips to exotic places you only read about. These are absolutely great aspirations if they add positively to your living experience. These types of descriptions, however, can fail to get you closer to the life that you truly desire.

Everyone, deep down, wishes to live a life that illustrates what's important to them. Millions have gotten swept up in the societal current of endless "doing." A six-figure salaried internet blogger wrote an article on people that brag on their busyness. He said, "A life full of too many things to do is quite frankly a disorganized life, and honestly nothing to brag about."

We as a collective must break free of this 'quantity over quality' approach to living. You may feel more connected to other busy people in your circle. Just remember much of your circle will probably go to their graves with regrets about what they wish they had done with their one life. In the end, we cherish the experiences we enjoyed rather than the number of tasks that we completed. Decide right now to be someone that took charge of life. Someone that placed their natural, God-given resources where they most mattered, instead of squandering these gifts in busyness.

There is a direct connection between the decisions we make and our quality of life. The big decisions aren't the ones that determine our paths. It's the little everyday clues that we decide to ignore. It is the way we waste our limited time on tasks that bring very little return on investment. It's the little lies we tell ourselves to do things we are in a habit of doing, though we know inside that it is a waste of time.

We See the Crack, and Yet We Still Fall Through: Value vs. Dream

Living a life created out of your values is actually your dream life. Living out of your values is the way you put your God-given resources to work to get what's important to you. Usually a picture of our dream life involves a money tree in our backyard. But much of what we believe is important to us is created out of what we don't have. When you never have enough, you will never have more. If you hold the belief that you lack money, your conscious dream will be large amounts of money. Then with large amounts of money you think about what bills you would pay, and what toys you would buy. You probably also think about what you would give to your family and charity. Yet we still haven't gotten to what's important to you. What are you called to do with your one life? What is your gift that you want to share with the world? Money may help you spread the answer to these questions, however, money is not the answer to these questions.

We are so consumed by our habit to look outside for answers that this basic principle escapes us. Constantly looking outside, our lives can resemble a hamster running on a wheel in a cage. That hamster may be moving fifty miles an hour. But if you leave the room and return, that same hamster will be in the exact same spot running on the same wheel. I don't know if the hamster gets worn out, but we do. So pictures of a dream life can show up in our heads as a never-ending vacation, an escape from the never-ending run on the wheel. Dreaming of an endless vacation may bring a smile to your face. Unfortunately the mental picture gets you no closer to a value-anchored life.

One of Mary Kay Ash's famous quotes is, "God first, family second, and career third." This is an example of her value-anchored life. These were the three elements most important to her, from which she derived her balance. You have to realize what is most important for you and create a life out of that. Otherwise you may exist, day to day, feeling overwhelmed and under-accomplished. This decision to find out what your values are inherently brings you from where you are to where you are really meant to be. You may even realize that you are presently where you want to be. And the discomfort or stress you have been placing on your life is a result of you allowing the expectations of others to influence your feelings, allowing what's outside of you to dictate what should be important to you. The advice to stick with your real job, instead of starting your business, is a great example. Either way, uncovering your values and living from that space will almost guarantee a life fulfilled.

Knowing your values creates naturally beneficial holistic goals. These goals instruct you on how to use your time. This is important because time, similar to oil, is a limited resource. Once it is gone, boys and girls, it's gone. We all have the same desire, which is to live the best life possible. To be successful, we must move from a 'quantity over quality' to a 'quality over quantity' position. Our activities must be consistent with what's important to us. Otherwise, the activity should be changed or stopped entirely. This way you can most certainly achieve a much better life.

Getting to "Best": There's No 'One Size Fits All,' Even When it Says So On the Pack

One great advantage of coaching is that you become conscious of your agenda. A coach's focus is squarely on you. In that space, the agenda is created and directed by you. For women, a coaching session may be the only time they solely focus on themselves. It is difficult, especially for women, to come face to face with what they want to do.

Women are constantly trying to balance their wants and desires with the wants and desires of those they care for most. We think, if I do "fill in the blank" for me, how will this affect my kids, husband, job performance, or family and friends? We think about everyone and everything else before we consider our personal desires, usually placing our needs at the bottom of the "To Do List," which becomes the "Never to Be List." Men, on the other hand, usually do what they want to do. Not because they love less, but because they place themselves at the top of the list.

Now, the first step to "Getting to Best" is going to be (of course) placing yourself at the very top of your "To Do List." There is a reason why, if there is an emergency on the plane and the oxygen masks drops down, you are instructed to give oxygen to yourself first: because if you die there's nothing you can do for anyone else. The moral to the story is to take care of you, if only to help those you love. Place you at the top of the list. This way, one thing is for sure – if nothing else gets done, you will. Here's the best part: once you begin to place yourself first, you will inevitably have more to give those that you love. You want to offer from the overflow of life's cup. Skipping your "pour" leaves you scrapping the bottom for what's left after everyone else has already gotten theirs. I don't know about you, but I don't want the bottom of anything. Therefore, if only to give more to those that you love, make the decision to place yourself on top.

"Getting to Best" is going to be different for each person because your idea of best and the next person's idea of best can be total opposites. Your life partner's idea of "Best" may differ from yours in some areas. That's why you must place yourself at the top of your list to uncover your real values. So no one else's values should get mixed in with yours. It's the placing ourselves last, and the mixing, that creates confusion and delusion. Remember what you most want (clarity) is already inside of you. There's nothing to discover, only to uncover.

There are different ways to uncover your values. You can, for example, write a list of what's important to you in your life. For some of you, this will take some time to complete. We are at different places on the value continuum. Or, as I like to say, various stage of disconnection from our true desires.

~ CHAPTER 6 ~

Everything I Know about Men

First of all, I would not know my daddy if he walked up to me on the street. So I had to learn about men through "on-the-job training," which was a haphazard affair to say the least. This is not to imply the learning has ended. Learning to be better is a lifelong commitment. Everyone would probably agree that hands-on-experience is great.

You usually have another person, preferably someone that knows more than you, showing you the ropes. These people are able to give you the benefit of his or her experience. They give you advice on what to look out for and what's the best way to succeed. They give you a real life example of what will be required to get where you want to go. These mentors let you know what worked for them, and more importantly what did not. Their knowledge shrinks your learning curve significantly and can propel you to years ahead of the game.

Now let's imagine the other side of on-the-job training. There's no one showing you the ropes (or no competent person showing you the ropes). You really want to be great in your position, but really have no idea how to be great.

There's no one to tell you what habits are essential in this "new job." No one to tell you what activities matter most, and what activities you can put on hold or not do at all. It's like trying to build a bridge with no one to guide you. Yes, you may have gone to school specifically to learn how to build bridges. But you have never seen it actually done in real life. So, although you have a learned set of instructions on how to build a bridge, you still shouldn't be left alone to build a bridge that's supposed to stand up.

This is how many of us learn about relationships with the opposite sex. We have an ingrained understanding of men because we were created to partner with them and make babies. That being said, without some quality directions on how to live happily with men or how to choose the right man, we can end up with babies and no daddies.

We are surrounded with examples of relationships. If you are lucky, some were good. With no filter, you have no idea what you should follow and what you shouldn't. You may have basic thoughts of what should happen in a good relationship. We want love, fidelity, and respect. Much like the bridge, you have no idea how to build these qualities in a real relationship. Often you have no one to tell you what works and what doesn't.

Instead, you are probably surrounded by people with no more knowledge of relationships than you. Yet they share their (frequently negative) opinions with or without being asked. You know who I'm talking about – your girlfriend that always has an opinion, yet almost never has a man. Or the girlfriend who does have a man, but you wouldn't want that type of relationship even if it came with a million dollar cash bonus.

The worst part about listening to these unqualified people is you are getting further away from what you want in your life: a happy, long lasting connection with another human being. Each bad relationship you have, partnered with the negative commentary, is leading you to believe that the right one is not out there, at least not for you.

You begin to create more anti-relationship habits, like long lists of crazy must-haves. Many of these must-haves are qualities you may not have yourself. Like when you demand that your man have a body builder's physique (though you are pleasingly plump in a couple of areas yourself). Or you want him to be the next Donald Trump (but your own finances could use a little attention). The other end of the spectrum is when we talk endlessly about what we don't want in a man. We don't want a man that cheats or lies to us. We don't want a man that doesn't have a professional career. Crazy lists of do's and don'ts are nothing more than defenses that we create to avoid being hurt once again.

Yet sooner or later we end up in the same type relationships that have failed in the past. Or we withdraw from the dating world altogether. This happens because we are stuck in patterns of behavior based on beliefs that aren't serving us. We developed these beliefs in reaction to relationships that we have seen at some point in our lives. The beliefs then become further cemented by our own experiences. So we get in this endless spiral of negative thinking and behavior until we consciously decide to be, and do, things differently to have a better result.

"You will never get more than what you are."

To have the meaningful relationships that our soul desires, we must decide to become what we desire from others. If you want to be loved, you must become more loving. But first, you must learn to love yourself truly, and then spread out that love to others.

When you really love yourself, you lose the need for lists altogether. Lists are a sign that you distrust yourself to do what's best for you. Loving you means knowing you will only choose the best. This doesn't mean you will automatically choose your soul mate tomorrow, but learning to love yourself does mean you will choose much better candidates for a soul mate in the future.

We Learn by Example

We teach people how to treat us by the way we treat ourselves. Our personal care provides a physical example and mental blue print for others to see. And I'm talking more than lipstick and nail polish, girls. Looking well-groomed on the outside is a nice start, but it's what you cultivate on the inside that attracts the good stuff. Your positive self-love gives off an invisible energy that attracts those with similar energy. This is why learning to truly love you is so important. You can't ask somebody to love you when you don't love you. Correction: you can ask anything, it just won't happen.

Create the Space: A Million Dresses and Not One to Wear

We all have that person in our lives, probably a young lady, who has four closets of clothes in her house. At the same time, whatever the event, she is buying a new frock to step out in. You, on the other hand, may wonder from time to time, "Why doesn't she just pull one of her million and one dresses out of the closet?" You have probably been a little nosey and poked around her closet just to prove your point and found unworn dresses with the tags firmly attached. Yet your friend seems to totally miss the fact that the dresses exist. Even if you pull out a dress to show her that she already has the perfect dress in her home, she will have one reason or another why it simply won't suit her purposes.

That example assumes that you are not the person with four closets of clothes. If you are that person, please don't get sensitive. This life lesson really has nothing to do with dresses (well, maybe a little). Clothes happen to be one of the numerous ways we fill up space. The reason she doesn't know the perfect dress is staring her in the face is because she really can't see it. Her view is muddled and cluttered with all the stuff in her way.

The first way to show love for you is to make the decision to de-clutter your life. Everything takes up space, whether it's physical objects or purely emotional. Therefore, whatever you want (in this case, love) needs its own spot. Anything you want to create or bring into your life is going to require a clear space to be appreciated. If you have a bunch of stuff or "dresses" cluttering your space, when love comes into your life you probably won't even know it's there.

Instead you will continue to go out collecting negativity and complaining that you aren't finding what you want: swearing up and down that what you do find is never quite what you want, or that Mr. Right ends up being Mr. Wrong. From there, you fill your closet with "clutter" – self-defeating thoughts and talks. You talk to yourself and all your (many times) equally sour girlfriends.

They share statements like, "I told you all men are dogs. Girl, you can't trust any man out here. All the good men are married already." Birds of a feather usually do flock together. So make sure you aren't perching with pigeons when you want to fly like a dove. You make up negative stories about what the failure of the relationship says about you, "It's me, and I just don't have good luck with men." And guess what, you are absolutely right. Whatever you believe and constantly affirm becomes the truth for you. Thankfully, we are in complete control of what we believe. So at any moment we can make a new decision to affirm a life condition that adds to our happiness instead of subtracting from it.

Stop the Chaos

Another form of clutter is chaos we allow to enter our lives. This means picking when we should be skipping. We fall into these habits of picking the same men over and over again. The names may vary but that's about all. Short or tall skinny or fat, it is the same man dressed in slightly different clothing. You know "Leroy" because he is in every state and every community in which you choose to reside. He possesses one (but probably more) of these characteristics: Leroy has kids by a few different mamas, is unemployed or under employed, and or doesn't show you the respect that he should. You find this out about him, and still stay in the relationship. Later, when everything plays out the way it was meant to, you get mad at poor Leroy. But we know that you are really mad at yourself. That's right, I said "Poor Leroy." He was just being himself when you wanted him to become somebody else.

A woman wrote to me with this question, "Why are abusive men attracted to me? I want to be in a relationship, but I'm tired of the drama." We as humans have an insatiable need to shift the responsibility of our lives to someone or something other than ourselves when something fails. We attempt to avoid the emotional pain that often accompanies self-inspection. This momentary pain, however, is necessary to reach the root of the problem: us. Because it is always us. We pick the people that spend time in our lives. Have you ever read, at the end of contest rules, "Many will enter few will win"? This sums up my point exactly – who approaches you really doesn't matter. Who enters the contest is who enters, but you alone are picking the winners. Your self-defeating energy will give you a higher percentage of undesirables than someone with positive "only the best for me" energy. In relationships, we all have received applicants that are "less than qualified for the position." The ones with great results just knew who to reject on the spot.

All the men that "Patricia," the woman who wrote in with her question, dates are pretty undesirable characters (I know because she included this information in her email). Their employment status is sketchy, they drink excessively, and are abusive either physically or verbally. Patricia believes these derelicts are cosmically drawn to her by some outside force. Remember, it's human nature to avoid blame at any cost. She decided to stop dating to solve the problem. She refused to even have coffee with anyone of the opposite sex for three years. Her girlfriends constantly attempt in vain to fix her up with their male friends. She claims to be happier alone than she has ever been in a relationship with someone.

One day, Patricia met a guy she felt instantly attracted to while out running errands. The stranger approached her, and they had a pleasant conversation. She still had reservations about entering into even a casual dating situation. Still, she continued to chat with her new friend and goes out on a few dates with him. She fell head over heels in love with, in her words, "a perfect guy." She believed faith has rewarded her dating abstinence with her dream man. Seven months later the relationship began to go south. Her present relationship started to resemble past encounters more and more with each passing day. She ultimately found herself in another negative "need to get out" or "get kicked out" relationship.

Does Patricia simply have terrible luck? No, Patricia followed the classic pattern of treating the symptoms and not the disease. She, and only she, is choosing these unworthy-of-her-affection mates. Her not dating solution provided a temporary plug to a much larger leak. You can duct tape a pipe (you shouldn't, but you can). When that water comes through, it's going to burst through….NOT drip through. Giving up dating made her think she was better. Her damaged self-esteem and her relationship habits were lying dormant waiting on her to make a move. Once she presented the opportunity with a new "Mr. Hell No," her patterns jumped into action. Some hedge all their bets on faith that everything will work out, completely ignoring freewill. Having faith that everything will turn out right when you are doing everything wrong is downright delusional. Blaming faith may momentarily exempt you from personal responsibility. Blaming faith will not stop the years of pain caused by active denial.

Finding and developing a plan to address personal issues is grueling work, but the reward of later finding a positive loving relationship is priceless. What activity on earth have you ever gotten better at without continuous focused practice? There is absolutely not one sport, profession, hobby, or academic subject I can name. Patricia's immediate halt to dating will stop her negative experiences for a while, but at what personal cost? An even better question is, how does the decision to cut herself off from the opportunity to love serve her?

~ CHAPTER 7 ~
Cursing the Blue Sky

The thing about being stuck in less than serving habits is that they are blind. These habits are reactive instead of responsive. When presented with an opportunity to shine, they jump into action without judging the situation, such as when you stumble upon that great man for you. It's a stumble because you are consciously picking men that are wrong. But for some reason, this time you decide to be different by doing different things to have something different. Maybe you are tired of past results and are truly ready to make a change in your life. So you go out with the guy that another day you would have turned down. He isn't any less attractive than the men you usually say yes to. He just doesn't feel like your usual type.

You say yes to his dinner invitation with a bit of hesitation. "To get something different, it is going to take doing something different," you think in your mind. You have probably come to this decision because you are sick and tired of being sick and tired. That's okay. Fatigue of the way life has been is the match to the dynamite in most of us. The point is to find purpose in your life, by getting to places within yourself where you can grow. Making the decision to do differently is the quickest road, in my opinion, to getting "on purpose" in any area of your life. Decisions are active. If you made a decision, you are presently moving on that decision. If you have a thought about what you want to do, but right now you are still sitting on the idea, you haven't made a decision. Sweetheart, you are just stalling to stay in your comfort zone. This is true in life and relationships, because staying where you are is so damn comfortable even when the situation is uncomfortable.

Now back to your new man (that you have hope will be different from the men you have chosen in the past). You have been going out for a few months and things have been going pretty well. This casual dating is beginning to resemble a full-fledge relationship. It is about now that you begin to have a nagging feeling that something isn't right. Or little things about him may start to get on your last available nerve. It could be the way he brushes his teeth in the morning that's irritating. He brushes right to left instead of left to right. You may begin to think that you are settling for someone that doesn't excite you, just to have a man in your life. All these self-defeating thoughts start to flood your less than certain brain.

So what do you do when this inevitable event takes place? You start sabotaging your otherwise good relationship. That's right, you start cursing your beautiful blue sky, which is one more way to clutter our space for love. There's not a rain cloud in sight as far as the eye can see, but this makes absolutely no impression on you, because you will paint a couple in yourself. I believe these sabotaging thoughts (not your actions) to be an inevitable occurrence whenever we do anything outside our comfort zone. I know right now you are thinking that you moved outside your comfort zone when you started dating this guy. You did take a giant step by opening this new door and walking through. Now, you have to make the decision to keep walking because each step ahead is going to bring a new discomfort. That's how growing works: if you are not experiencing some level of discomfort in your life's activities, please choose a few new activities that stretch you, because you will only grow stronger through being stretched.

I am not telling you this new man is your soul mate sent down from heaven specifically for you. I don't know if he is or isn't, but you probably have no idea either. I am telling you to give the current good man (or the good man you will choose in the future) a fighting chance. You do this by becoming aware that these thoughts, which will lead to feelings, are going to enter your mind. This is your mind trying to pull you back to where everything is warm and familiar. But you have decided to forego warm and familiar for growing to get new and better. This will be your choice in the areas of your life where you decide to have more. Decisions are important, not because we always make the right ones, because you won't. Decisions are important because you are moving, and once you are moving you can adjust.

Rub His Nose in the Mess

An aunt of mine once owned the cutest puppy in the world. She was a mixed breed, otherwise known as a mutt. "Lady" had big beautiful brown eyes with a matching cream-colored coat. She licked the faces of everyone she met, even complete strangers. The little dog was perfect in every way, except for one minor flaw: she would not go potty properly. My aunt loved Lady but loved a clean house more than just about anything in the world. Clorox bleach was her main cleaning product and the smell was the only air freshener she needed. Therefore, continuous doggy bathroom accidents on her spotless floors were completely unacceptable. Aunt Lisa rubbed her dog's nose in the urine each time she used the kitchen floor as her own personal bathroom. Still, the dog never learned to only go when outside (at least with my aunt). Failing to properly train Lady, Lisa gave the puppy away to a close friend of hers.

Not very long ago, rubbing a dog's nose in his own waste to teach him or her proper bathroom etiquette was an acceptable practice. Many animal owners believed this form of negative reinforcement to be an effective training method. These days, countless animal owners have rejected this method as a way to get desired results. This may have been a common practice yesterday, but these animal owners are choosing new ways today. In math, a negative multiplied by a negative does provide a positive result. In real life, pouring in negativity rarely produces a positive outcome. Yet many of us react to less than pleasing actions by others with additionally less than pleasing actions. We do what we have learned to do, regardless of our real world results. It's hard to get better results from a person if you keep pointing out what's bad. This as a regular practice will build frustration and, over a long period of time, even contempt on both sides of the relationship.

I had to remind myself of this simple truth quite recently during a conversation with my husband. He is notorious for his commitment to home improvement projects. Honestly, he is an absolute genius when it comes to doing this type of work. He can remodel an entire kitchen after reading a couple of home improvement books like a pro. This is an awesome asset, but quickly completing a project is not his forte. He will tear down an entire room of kitchen cabinets in a few hours. He will dig out an unhealthy shrub or plant without me asking twice. One problem – he often gets bored with the improvement element of his improvement projects. He is most interested in the demolition part of home improvement projects. As a Success Coach, I appreciate the spiritual and psychological value of an organized, clutter-free space. In the past, on a good day, I have chosen to ignore his "Bob the Destroyer" habits. On a less than good day….well, let's just stay in positive territory. My problem is that I would attempt to rub his nose in the mess. Like my aunt with her puppy (except my husband is a person), I wanted my husband to conform to me. I wanted him to quickly finish his projects to get my orderly house back, like my aunt wanted her clean floors. So how did I work to accomplish this lofty goal? I nagged him relentlessly with the hope that he would concede.

I would ask in my 'outside' voice, "Why do you begin projects that you have no intention of finishing?"

He would reply with, "I am going to finish, you need to have a little more patience."

Remember, a negative multiplied by a negative equals more negativity in the real world. This back and forth went on for years between us. One day I looked at one of his latest unfinished projects, ready to begin our usual sparring match, when suddenly, the phrase, "This is getting you absolutely nowhere" popped into my head. Say something today that's different from yesterday, I thought. I decided to implement a more positive approach. Instead of getting angry over the multiple unfinished projects, I offered to help him complete them. To date, we have more completed projects than incomplete. I also learned that we work really well together. Yes, I do have home improvement projects that have not crossed the finish line but that's okay. There are now fewer messes to clean up and I didn't have to rub his nose in any of them.

Negative thinking creates clutter in your brain and spirit, which lead to you taking the wrong actions. Work to remain positively focused in every area of your life. Positive focus means working toward what you want, rather than dwelling on what you don't want or don't have. This creates a propelling energy that will serve as motivation for you. Ask yourself often, "What can I do right now to positively affect this situation?" Sometimes what you will be able to do will be a lot and sometimes it will be a little. Decide in your heart right now that it all matters, because it does.

Old Habits Only Die if You Kill Them; Monkey Do Monkey See

In the immortal words of the famous G.I. Joe cartoon, "Knowing is half the battle." Yet knowing, for many of us, is the complicated part of the life equation. We walk around thinking negative situations just appear in our lives, and may even tell ourselves we have "bad luck." I am here to tell you, the idea of good luck vs. bad luck does not exist – only choice and response. This is true in real life as well as intimate relationships. You choose the people with whom you become involved. Most of us, in this modern day, can freely choose our partners. Some individuals choose well and others less well. Often we fail to respond correctly to our poor choices, and fall into a habit of doing the same things over and over again.

Most of our habits, and in this case relationship habits, are learned behaviors we picked up from parents or others close to us. This is true even when we label our parents and other influential couples as "less than desirable" examples to follow. We do what we know to do, so what happens if what you know to do is wrong? You will continuously take the wrong actions and experience the same wrong results.

My mother has never been in a good, long-term intimate relationship. Although otherwise assertive, I never felt she demanded enough from her partners. I remember being about ten years old and eaves-dropping on a conversation she was having with my siblings' father. He had been MIA for several weeks, which was nothing out of the ordinary, and now talking his way back into her life. "Maria, I don't deserve to be with you, because I'm a mess, but I just can't live without you," blah blah blah.

I give Wilfred an E for effort; he should have taken his act to Hollywood and made some money. He was always quite convincing with his tears and perfectly positioned pauses. One time, when Mama was especially fed up with his BS, Wilfred decided to tragically kill off his oldest son from a previous relationship. No, he didn't actually murder his son. He did tell

Mama that he had died in some sort of sudden accident. This was a lie he stuck to for a few years, until he finally admitted the truth.

So, what is the lesson I learned from my relationship example? Well, first it's important to note that I wasn't immediately aware that I had formed certain thoughts as a result of my model. Many of our lessons are learned completely unconsciously. You hear or see something and formulate a belief, or adjust what you observed to fit an existing belief. This process occurs every day in our lives without us even realizing. I never considered what was the wrong type or the right type of man to love. In my mind, Mama merely needed to lay down an ultimatum and she would have gotten everything she wanted out of the relationship.

I identified the problem partially, but I had not found a real solution. Demanding more from your mates does not mean you can force another person to do anything. First of all, attempting to force a man (child or adult) to do anything is impossible. You can trust my words: I have seven siblings, three children, and a husband. It does mean, though, you will not continue to have a relationship with anyone that does not meet your needs.

As a result of this totally unconscious view, I entered relationships thinking I could control the actions of the other person. Needless to say, I was unsuccessful and could not seem to let the relationships die natural deaths because of the beliefs I held. Most of the relationships you have are supposed to end, because they are just valuable practice. The relationships we have allow us to figure out our true partner needs. Dating cuts out the possibilities, and returns certainties.

For example, you may think you want the next Donald Trump of the world, which is great. You need to be absolutely clear on what type of individual becomes the "Donald." This type of man or woman will spend most of their time working, especially in the beginning. Therefore, their time with you will be extremely limited and often interrupted. So you need to be aware that many good traits have drawbacks as well.

Keeping your focus on being clear will save you a lot of pain in the long term. I became obsessed with not repeating the mistakes of my mother. So, of course, I began to repeat the mistakes of my mother. I wasn't clear on what type of relationship I wanted to have. Every time my brain thought of a good relationship, by default it spat out "don't wants." Focusing on what you do not want doesn't get you to what you do. Energy goes where focus flows, period. Our lives are largely a reflection of our most frequent thoughts.

You want a loving, supportive, faithful man to come into your life. Think about that type of man coming into your life. Right now, you're thinking "Whatever, it's not that easy." You are right – change is a common challenge. That being said, the benefits you will receive far outweigh the momentary discomfort or growing pain. Learning a new skill is a change, yet we learn new skills to enhance our lives financially, physically, or emotionally. Thinking positively or, as I like to say, thinking from an "empowered position" is a new skill that will deeply enhance your life where ever and whoever you are.

My thoughts of "I will be different from her if I can just make the relationship work" lacked empowerment. Of course, at some point I freed myself from this unfortunate pattern. But what should be the next step to insure that I never find myself in this place again?

First, you must provide yourself with a clean "work space." Past relationships are not indicators of your future. It is impossible to create a new beginning while holding tightly to an unchangeable past. Next, I confronted my fear of possibly following in my mother's footsteps. No dwelling, just a quick acknowledgement. We are all navigators of our own destinies, and our fears alone lead us to believe otherwise. I got eye to eye with myself and declared that it was my divine birthright to be treated exceptionally. God never makes junk, and he didn't start with me. He only creates fine China that must be handled with care. I also stopped talking about men in negative terms to my girlfriends. It's impossible to think positivity and talk negativity at the same time. You are throwing out the good with the bad while asking for better. Much like oil and water, the two just don't mix. Finally, I promised myself to seek the advice of an objective party when in doubt. Sometimes we become desensitized by past experiences, and therefore are unable to distinguish between healthy and unhealthy relationships. There's everything right about asking someone you admire for their advice in an area where they have knowledge.

My Life, My Invention, or Why the Big Toe?

Positivity always begins with a foundation rooted in productive thinking. Productive thinking is any thoughts that are internally inspiring and lead to immediate action. When you are internally inspired, your external environment will instantly improve. These improvements are not always big earth-shattering improvements. But for every step I take in a positive direction, there seems to be at least one more step added to mine. Every morning, I am thankful to my God that he awakened me. That first positive thought takes me directly to the next positive thought. I am thankful for the love of my family. The positivity continues from one thought to the next, until I am completely overwhelmed by the large number of my blessings. My existence is too positive, too positively focused, to become negative. All my thoughts are focused on everything to be accomplished. Negative thoughts take an opposite path. Once the first perceived negative instance happens, the entire day seems to follow.

Here's an example: Tasha gets up later than she usually does to get ready for work. She is immediately annoyed at her limited preparation time. Why did I get up so late? Now, I am forced to rush out the door today. She agonizes over her tardiness the entire drive to work, "Man, I'm going to be a full half hour late." Tasha is beginning her day with pure negativity. What is the point? Time travel has not been invented. Therefore, she is unable to travel back in time and change the present. Let it go! Move on sweetheart! Her entire day is going to be filled with negative experiences. She began forming her day with that first thought. Right now, her day is unfolding exactly in the manner she created in her mind.

Think about those times when you rolled out of bed, took two steps, and stubbed your toe in the morning. Immediately you declare that it isn't going to be a good day. You might have said this with actual words, thoughts, or both. Then the entire day seems to follow a pattern of negative occurrences. At the end of the day, you proudly profess, as if the prize were something other than your own unhappiness, "I knew it was going to be a bad day when I stubbed my toe, especially the big toe. That's the toe that hurt the worst." You might not express yourself in those words exactly, but words quite similar. We blame an entire day, and often our entire lives, if we remain unaware of the positives.

We become convinced that our experiences are beyond our control. Tasha's life, like everyone else that breathes, is her own invention. She has the power to turn her day around in this very moment. Her day can go from bad to outstanding in a single instant with a single change of thought. I know what you might be thinking, "This is some old think-happy-thoughts, and be happy nonsense." No, I am suggesting something much greater than a feel good regimen. Yes, goal boards and personal mission statements are all excellent tools to use on the journey of self-improvement. These tools, however, are worthless without a concrete belief that you are indeed the master of your faith. You cannot stop the rain from falling when it does, but you can decide to be your own umbrella.

"Being happy doesn't mean everything is perfect. It means you have decided to look beyond the imperfections." ~ Unknown

A belief system is the deciding factor in genuine self-improvement. It allows you to create a positive focus when positive thoughts are out to lunch because there's nothing positive about the situation. This is the case when we lose our loved ones or develop an illness. Mustering up some positive thoughts may be a stretch. Yet a positive focus is always within reach when you have the belief that you control your response. You can decide to use the illness as an opportunity to improve your physical fitness, from what you eat to what you do. This can be the time in your life when important relationships get the attention you always wanted to give, but felt you couldn't spare before. You can decide to take up a cause that was important or somehow connected to your lost loved one. This may be the fire under your feet to start living full out because, as the great motivator Les Brown says, "It's later than you think."

Sure, we may do the physical work involved in creating mission statements, or even follow affirmations for a while. Nonetheless, real personal enhancement will not occur until a belief system that is grounded in personal control exists. All of us have been really excited about one goal or another at some point. Possibly going back to school, starting a new career, living a more balanced life, etc. We were really excited and somehow it just doesn't happen. Why? Our deepest beliefs prevent us from accomplishing our goals. In your head you're saying, "Yes, this is my time." Right when you're most excited, you hear a second voice whisper, "Who are you kidding? That's never going to happen." The whisper is your innermost beliefs talking you out of persistently pursuing your purpose.

You act on whatever the subconscious whisper is saying to you, and you ignore the suggestions from your screaming conscious mind. Why? The subconscious mind contains thoughts that you feel so deeply that the thought becomes buried within your brain. Conscious thoughts lay on the surface, so they can be here today, gone tomorrow. But the whispers are currently held internalized beliefs. For this reason, even when we act on the thoughts of our conscious minds our results can be less than stellar. Actions that lack belief is like driving with no destination in mind – you're moving but you aren't getting anywhere.

~ CHAPTER 8 ~

It Ain't What You do, It's What You Think

W orking in sales is the greatest job in the world for thousands of people. These people enjoy a pay system directly tied to performance. Others reluctantly agree to a job in sales when no other offers are presently available. In college, a particular soft drink company hired lots of their employees from my alma mater. Some were excited at the opportunity to work for such a successful company, and others were underwhelmed even at the prospect to elevate their title and compensation without being required to obtain an MBA. Two classmates of mine landed jobs with the popular beverage company.

Both men were excited about the impressive compensation structure. You received a great base salary plus bonuses and were placed on a sales management track. Steve could not contain his excitement about the opportunity. He said it is pretty much guaranteed that if you stay with the company for two years you will be a sales manager. Your salary instantly jumped another

$20,000 and you received higher bonuses. Brian's opinion of being offered such a position seemed lukewarm at best. He acknowledged that the pay was above average, coming straight out of college, and that's pretty much where the enthusiasm stopped. He had no interest in becoming a manager because, according to him, "They're going to just put you in a hick town in the middle of nowhere." It was simply impossible to get a positive statement from this guy. Brian literally began to complain even before he officially began the job.

Steve excelled in his sales position and always exceeded the expected quota. Brian never failed to just barely make his numbers. He complained about disgruntled storeowners and being required to maintain displays. The market they worked in was one of the most lucrative areas in the nation at the time. Still, Brian blamed everything but himself for his inability to move product. The two men had two completely different accounts of the exact same job, dealing with the exact same people. Brian admitted to never wanting to work in sales as a career and thought the job beneath him. He said to me once, "I expected to be doing something more with my degree. Begging storeowners to buy soda is not my idea of a dream job." His lack of desire to work in sales was a little puzzling, because he holds a BS in Marketing. Most marketing jobs are in, you guessed it, sales. His goals were obviously misaligned with his actions or he never created any goals to align. In truth, Brian's lack of defined goals was the least of his problems. His negative state of mind is what hurt him the most.

Brian actually visited a lot more stores than Steve, but his order requests were never nearly as high. He approached vendors with an already defeated, "Sorry to bother you," attitude. Living in the United States provides unlimited opportunities in just about everything, so there is no accounting for a poor attitude. Thomas Jefferson was correct when he said, "Nothing can stop the man with the right mental attitude from achieving his goal; nothing on earth can help the man with the wrong mental attitude." The right attitude in life is absolutely mandatory to be successful, because attitude is what creates perceptions. Our perceptions paint pictures in our minds that we act upon. These pictures and subsequent actions become our reality.

Brian's conscious mind may have decided he would accept the job – his subconscious mind had not agreed, and it is our subconscious that has to grant permission. We all have at some point planned to do something important to us, maybe go back to school or buy a house. We affirmed, in our conscious mind, "This will absolutely happen." Yet somehow we simply don't follow through with our plan. Why? You may think "Yes, I can," but if your subconscious whispers "No, you can't," then no, you won't. Like Brian, your body will show up to the event and your subconscious will do all the talking.

Your subconscious mind is what you really believe is possible, regardless of what you actually do. Therefore your mind uses these often subconscious beliefs to draw pictures in your head of what you can and cannot do. Case in point, Brian visited more stores than Steve in a given week. Yet his sales told a very different story. The picture in his head was of him "begging," as he put it, storeowners. Begging implies someone taking pity on you or giving you some form of charity. He was selling a product that millions of consumers drink every day. Not to mention, he was selling this product in one of the company's most profitable markets. Obviously there was a lot of demand for what he was offering. Let's add in, his colleague was making more going to fewer stores.

The reality is that there was great money to be made, he just wasn't making it, went clean over his head. Yes, he was showing up asking for a "Yes" but seeing a "No" in his head, which is exactly what he received. This is why what you believe is more important than how you act. Now here's where it gets interesting. You can use your actions to change what you believe. I know, right now it sounds like a contradiction. It sounds like doubletalk because I said what you believe is more important than what you do. But we are all familiar with the cliché of "Fake it till you make it." You can act like what you wish to believe. As I mentioned before, I prefer to think of it as "Practice," but the other one is more catchy.

The Power of Self-Talk

Thousands of people attend motivational seminars each year with short term, or worse, no significant increase in motivation level. They go in earnestly looking for ways to improve their lives through positive thinking. There is no lack of desire on their part, merely lack of an essential tool. They are missing the "Power of Self-Talk," which is an absolute requirement in any successful endeavor. It is the power of self-talk alone that has the strength to change the subconscious mind.

We are all a sum of parts developed over a period of years. This is true whether you are one or 100 years old. The building of your subconscious mind begins the very moment you open your eyes for the first time as an infant. These forever accumulating parts are the very foundation of our subconscious thinking process. A motivational lecture alone will not change a thought process in a few hours that has taken a lifetime to build. Thoughts that have penetrated deep enough to reach the subconscious must be removed through consistent conscious effort. Your brain is trained to reject any idea outside of its belief structure. A person will believe all notions that comply with their beliefs regardless of rationality. On the other hand, all the evidence in the world will not convince someone whose subconscious mind believes otherwise.

Mr. Brown lived three blocks down the street from my family's home. He was an extremely friendly, always upbeat neighbor. I referred to him as "salt and pepper man" behind his back, because the two mixed together looked much like his hair. Salt and pepper never appears to be a real gray. You can distinctly see what's black and what's white, just like his hair. Mr. Brown would stop and talk to Mama just about every day on his way to the corner store. He was in his fifties and had never had a wife or children. In his own words, "I am a lifelong lover of freedom. "Don't wanna be tied to no woman telling me what to do and when to do all the time. And definitely no screaming kids running around driving me crazy"

In what seemed to be an outright contradiction to his life's choices, he loved being an uncle and would have his nieces and nephews over often. Some were around my age and we would play together. Mr. Brown had a particularly aggressive "Just do whatever needs to be done" attitude. He felt political leaders could actually improve the world instead of just maintaining if they stopped pussy footing. His position: "Jump off a plane this minute and you will learn to land on your way down." He employed this line of thinking in all parts of his life, because it was part of his belief structure.

Mr. Brown claimed to be an absolutely competition-caliber swimmer. He had learned to swim in a manner that was consistent with his attitude of jumping into a situation and figuring out the rest. This is an excellent practice in areas of life without deep bodies of water. Growing up in rural Louisiana had helped to feed this mentality. There were not many formal avenues to take if you desired to learn the most traditional of activities, such as swimming. Mr. Brown said there were no pools or swim instructors where he lived. There was the mighty Mississippi river and your wish to learn. According to Mr. Brown, he jumped in the river one hot summer afternoon and began to swim. He advocated this style as the most effective way in which to learn, because you will be forced to swim, or you will most certainly drown. Fear of imminent death would be the fire under your backside propelling you forward. He boasted that he had taught his own relatives by throwing them into deep water and turning his back.

One summer, his niece (Denice) must have listened a bit too closely to her uncle. She was at a pool party thrown by friends when she abruptly jumped into the deep end of the pool. No one went in behind her because they all thought she could swim. Why else would she jump into eight feet of water when she was only five feet tall? At first, her friends believed she was attempting to scare them when she didn't immediately come back up to the top. Luckily, one of the parents was not convinced she was joking, and went into the pool after her. Denice survived her impromptu pool lesson that summer.

I asked Denice later what her uncle said after the swimming incident. "The first thing he asked, so, do you know how to swim?" Denice's near death experience was not enough to change his thought process. Neither his love for his niece, nor her near death experience, had any impact on his internalized belief system.

~ CHAPTER 9 ~

The Problem with Fighting Over Scraps Is, Sooner or Later You're Going to End Up Hungry

A while ago, there was a story in the news about a woman who won a brand new home. The lucky lady also received an additional $500,000 to pay the property taxes, and a new SUV to get around. The winner appeared absolutely elated. She spoke extensively about how much living in the city, where the home was located, would benefit her autistic adult son. He was a student at a local community college pursuing an associate degree in art. The family's new city apparently had a well-developed art scene that would allow him to further his artistic talents.

Readers could leave comments in response to the article if they liked. The first few were really quite positive. Some of the readers simply congratulated the lucky lady and wished her all the best. Others said, "She has won nothing but a headache that will leave her in debt," or other, similarly negative comments. The comments became more and more negative as you continued down the list. Many responders actually wrote it would have been better for her to have never won the house. They cited everything from property taxes to maintenance. The depth of the negativity could choke you, as if someone actually had hands around your neck.

Sure, the taxes on the home are very expensive, and we have not begun to discuss utilities or upkeep. That being said, she won a brand new home, people. She could sell the house at a discounted price if needed, and walk away with over a million dollars. How can anyone turn that into a terrible misfortune of fate? Sadly, negative thinking can turn the most positive event in the world into someone's worst nightmare. These thoughts will pick away at the human spirit until there is nothing left to salvage. Negativity is akin to a weed; it will spring up out of nowhere and spread uncontrollably. Those affected walk around in a forever broken and beaten state. They are confrontational, edgy, nervous, and view all events (good or bad) as one more slight. Many of us unconsciously fall into the trap of negative thinking. Things we see in the news, death of a loved one, our personal choices, or any other stressful life event can lead you into the awaiting jaws of unhappiness. Here are three characteristics of negative thinking to avoid.

1. Complaints and Ain'ts

Complaining is a method used to excuse the act of doing nothing to solve the problem at hand. Unfortunately, the more you complain, the more powerless you feel. Complaining destroys self-reliance and throws you deeper into self-pity. Stop complaining in its tracks. Immediately think something positive about the situation or your ability to handle the situation.

Secondly, focusing on what you aren't (or "ain't") going to do is just as harmful. It is simply impossible to solve a problem from the inside. You must step outside and figure out what you do want. Then and only then can you figure out how to get it.

2. Rescue Me

Never ever turn yourself into a helpless victim endlessly searching for a rescue from life. These people blame others and circumstances for their current position. They refuse to accept responsibility for the condition of their lives. Sitting around waiting for a rescue is a waste of your limited time on earth. You are the only one with the ability to change your life for the better. A woe-is-me attitude will provide short-term excuses with long-term negative implications. Self-responsibility is the only way to safe guard against a "victim mentality."

A friend lost his job in the recent economic downturn. His first words after losing his job were, "I now look at CNBC every day, and the station announced a threat of recession several months before it occurred. Next time, I will develop a plan to lessen the impact of a possible job loss." Every experience we have is a lesson, and every lesson provides empowering information. Victims never absorb empowering information because they reduce their lives down to random acts of nature in which they have no control. These people live their lives in weighted agony. Ordinary daily events become additional bars added to their already mentally heavy existence.

3. Stinking Thinking

Our very thoughts create the world we see around us. People who suffer from continuous negative thinking perceive the world as grim and miserable. They attract others who share their views because no one else will tolerate their relentless pessimism. Our friends are a direct reflection of who we are at that moment. Positive individuals hang out with other positive individuals. Negative friends will reinforce your self-destructive attitude. The absence of positive energy will rob you of focus, a desire to persevere, and a productive life. Keep negative thoughts out of your mind by filling it with real positivity. Affirmations alone will not improve your primary thought process. Chanting "I am happy" affirmations can only work if your beliefs are strong. Develop a happy belief system by being grateful for everything presently in your life every day.

Consistently replace negative feelings with positive images, and your belief system will believe you.

Living a successful life is a direction, not a destination. Never allow yourself to become hung up on a specific idea. Ideas are nothing more than pebbles on the road. Some are gold, others silver, and some are just sign posts to keep walking. The key is to remain on the same road until successful.

Thousands of us human beings have an innate fear of failing. We allow this fear to dictate our lifestyle choices often in a self-limiting way. There are moments in life where fear is actually a good thing. For example, if you were standing on the edge of a thirty story building, fear would be your body telling you to come down before you fall to your death. A little fear is necessary in all meaningful endeavors. Side note: the avoidance of falling to your death is an extremely meaningful endeavor. I always feel a little nervous when giving a speech, regardless of whether or not it's live or a recorded audio. This fear helps me to study and prepare at sometimes insane levels. These practices insure that I always perform at my absolute best.

On the flip side, too much fear can completely immobilize the best-laid plans. I am referring to fear of doing things that will not end in physical injury of any sort. The fear of failure stops many from taking a calculated risk. You say to yourself, "What if I fail, then what?" Then, you get up and dust your pants or skirt off, and continue onward. Never fret over tweaking the original plan a little here and there. The true plan is to walk in the direction of success, and the individual ideas are merely possible routes. Routes provide opportunities to get going and move in the right direction, which ultimately leads to success.

Someone very close to me dreamed of founding a record company to showcase the talent of his artists. Derick had one big investor in his larger than life dream: himself. He, in his little one bedroom apartment, recorded the music of his artists. His small walk-in closet became an even smaller sound booth, and every inch of his living space served a musical purpose. He had no money for lawyers to incorporate the business or copyright his original work. There were no expensive studio engineers to record his music. Therefore, he did what every committed person does to fulfill his dreams. Mr. Derick found a way to incorporate, copyright and record his own material. When he did have the money to go to the music studio, he knew almost as much about recording as the professionals. He even began recording other artists for the music studio owner in exchange for studio recording time.

He couldn't play a single note on his $3500 keyboard that he bought with his entire earnings from working outside in sometimes one hundred degree heat on the railroad one summer. He just knew his artists needed music to accompany their vocals, and allowed the rest to take care of itself. I asked, "Why did you buy an expensive instrument you couldn't play?"

His answer? "I intended to find someone who could."

When you have a strong enough "Why?" trust me, the how will appear. Three months after purchasing the keyboard, he found someone who could play, and with his guidance, created original music. I remember hearing Tony Robbins say on one of his CDs, "It's never a lack of resources, it's always a matter of resourcefulness."

The truth is, you will find a way to accomplish whatever is a priority to you. Everything in your life that you currently possess, at least the things that weren't handed to you, were a priority for you. We act on our priorities. Goals that become priorities get done. Barely in his twenties, Derick had taken full musical responsibility for over ten acts. At the time, Derick was still in college working on his degree in finance. He was either in class or working with his multiple artists. All of his money from summer and part-time jobs went straight into his business. Creating a record company to showcase his musicians became his singular focus.

He had successes with his music business, even signed a deal with a famous record company. Some of his artists, however, began to leave or their level of commitment to their craft changed. He began to consider whether or not he wanted to continue in the music industry. His family was hounding him to give up the music to work a regular job. He asked my opinion. I said to him, "It is better to live part of your life following your dream, than to live your whole life following someone else's." Derick and Derick alone had to decide if he had found gold, silver, or just a pebble on the road. In the end, he decided to shut down his record company. He had mixed feelings regarding the end of what had been his dream for a number of years.

After the music, he worked as a financial aid counselor at a local state college for a couple of years. His salary was extremely low. Government workers are not usually the highest paid individuals. The hours were long and he did the paperwork for a few thousand students. We have even not begun to discuss how face-to-face meetings and weekend phone calls to his numerous students were a requirement. No overtime was offered because he was paid on salary, which is also known as **Stay As Late As Required, Yes Sir**. Derick, needless to say, was less than enthused about his new employment position though he never complained and felt thankful to have a job where he made a difference. I personally met several of the students he worked with, and they all raved about how much he helped them. His gratitude for the opportunity provided to him, especially in a down economy, was immense. Real gratitude allows you to be appreciative of what you have presently, and opens you up to receive more down the road.

He never forgot all that he had accomplished with little to no resources in his music company. Derick decided to step out on faith, and leave his position as a financial aid counselor. We had discussed the pros and cons of his leaving for months. The final decision to quit his job was made in a moment one night. The very next day he handed in his two weeks' notice, and began clearing out his office. Real definitive decisions are made in a moment and then are followed by immediate action. Talking about what you are going to do isn't taking action; it is just a stalling tactic. You will turn around, and you will only now be acting on a decision you talked about five years ago. Time passes quickly and standing still seems to speed it up.

For a few months, he survived on some savings from a retirement account from his former job. Each day that passed with no employment prospects only increased his urgency. Surprisingly, Derick never questioned if leaving was the best decision. Win or win another day, you must stand steadfast in your decision. Feel good that you made the best decision for you at the time by acting on the knowledge you possessed.

Just as the savings were running out, he received a phone call from a cousin. There was a temporary job available as a driver for a telecom contractor. Basically, he would taxi around an engineer for a cell phone company. He did some research and found engineers commanded a salary at the low end of $40,000 a year which is almost twice what he made as a financial aid counselor. At the high end, you could make up to $100,000 a year. On that knowledge alone, he took the job as a glorified cab driver.

Just about all the people who earn the title of engineer have a degree in engineering, not finance, and years of experience. Derick stayed at work hours after his shift had ended to learn telecom. He read every book he could lay his hand on that explained the mechanics of the industry. Other drivers, some with engineering degrees, attempted to discourage him with statements like, "This is a hard industry to advance in, and we have engineering experience and are still drivers." He ignored all of these "boo hoos." Derick said he would become an engineer and within two years he was not only an engineer, a career he loves, he is also one of the best paid and has been promoted another level up on the engineering tier.

The confidence he gained through the development of his music company is priceless. He worked twenty-four hours a day following his passion without making a dime. So, he looked at the opportunity to get into telecom as being paid to learn. It would have been easy to lose faith in what he could accomplish after the closure of his business. Yet, he used the experience as proof of his vast capabilities. Some of his present colleagues think he is lucky to have advanced so quickly. Wise people know in life there is little unearned luck. There is willful determination meeting opportunity. Individuals that consistently employ their "willful determination" just appear lucky.

When something isn't working, change your approach to the situation, but stay in the direction of success until you succeed. Derick chose not to sit in a corner and complain about what could have been. He wasn't even sure of what his next step in life would include. He pointed himself in the direction of success and was prepared for an opportunity when it arose.

~ CHAPTER 10 ~

Yes Sir, Only the Best for Me—You Will Never Achieve More Than Your Own Expectations

I remember first starting on the journey of self-improvement as a method to "Become my Potential." There were countless publications explaining in one way or another that you must have unwavering "determination" to succeed. Strong determination creates persistence to work until your goal is fulfilled. Some authors describe determination as being "hungry" to accomplish your goals. Now, all that sounded great and the information made absolute sense to me. Still, I was puzzled as to how you develop "lasting determination."

First let's define the word "determination." There are a few different definitions. My personal preference is Dictionary.com's entry: "Determination is the act of coming to a decision or of fixing or settling a purpose." Just from the definition we know determination or "hunger" is active. Therefore, being determined is going to require movement. Okay, it's pretty easy to motivate yourself to act for a few weeks, a few months, even a year. How do you move on your dreams everyday with the realities of life all around you? Just living through everyday life can be quite challenging at times.

So here's what creates "lasting determination:" real expectations. Yes ladies and gentlemen, it is simply impossible to sustain determination without strong expectations. Let's examine why unwavering expectations are essential to lasting determination. All the actions we take are based on an expectation of some improved return. You work a job with the expectation of getting paid for your labor. No matter how much you love that job, you would take your talents somewhere else if you weren't getting a check. You date with the expectation of finding a person or persons (depending on how you roll) with whom to spend time. Expectations are what keep us engaged in whatever we are doing.

Let's face it, becoming your potential is usually going to require some hard work. If getting to where you are meant to be were easy, you would already be there. Developing new skills will be a requirement just to apply for the position. You are going to have to love being uncomfortable, because hard work dictates discomfort. Sorry, willpower or the ability to suck it up will not do in this case. Sheer willpower uses up too much energy. You ultimately will get worn out and give up, or when you reach your goal it hardly seems worth the effort. You must develop the perspective that the silver lining in all this hard work is you will develop qualities in this process you never imagined or even considered for yourself. The quality of life you will experience pursuing your greatness will far outweigh any momentary discomfort. This, my friends, is the power of positive expectations.

When you have solid expectations for yourself, there are no alternatives to winning. The word "Win" is the most important word in your vocabulary. You expect to accomplish your goals wholeheartedly, without doubt, and at the same time are willing to make adjustments on the route along the way, if necessary. Regardless of what the unending tides of life bring to your doorstep, these goals become imprinted on your soul, and are as realistic to you as taking your next breath. Expectations allow you to look past circumstances and toward possibility. The decision to take this position in life gives energy instead of siphoning it off.

The first step in creating rock solid expectations is to concentrate your focus. This area will demand the most effort. Many of us allow beliefs and environment to dictate where we focus our thinking energy. We freely abdicate our focused attention to the calling of the moment, and later wonder why our lives appear to be disjointed messes.

Almost all of us hold on to beliefs that no longer serve us – beliefs that, if unchanged, will block your path to greatness. Discarding outworn beliefs is where you will do the most work. Beliefs systems act as our guideposts to living. Desires that fit into our current belief structure get acted upon immediately without a second thought. That's great if you have no wish to raise your personal life standard. If you want to step into your greatness by becoming your potential, some fundamental beliefs are going to have to change. Otherwise your goals will never get out of the starting gate.

If You Never Move Farther, You Get Stuck Where You Are

A college professor gave our business class a lecture on how our life priorities are born. He, too, believed that much of who we are, and what we demand from life is developed in childhood. According to him, "If you grow up hungry, you will work to keep yourself fed," and "If you grow up without clothes, you will work to wear the nicest fashions," and "If you grow up rich, you will work to become richer." What you focus your attention upon consciously or unconsciously becomes your priority. Unconscious negative focus is the worst, because you keep banging your head against a wall you are unable to see.

A friend of mine talked of seldom receiving presents and new clothes each year during her childhood. She grew up poor with two brothers in a single parent household. Yet, her poverty isn't the main reason she didn't receive gifts. Her oldest brother had been frequently incarcerated most of his adult life. She and I had been friends for five years prior to me ever seeing Troy face to face. Amber told me once that her mother used their Christmas money each year to give the brother something extra in prison. Therefore, Amber and her little brother would spend every holiday season wishing for at least one gift.

Amber would receive two pairs of pants and three new shirts each school year. A new pair of shoes depended upon how worn out the ones from the previous year were. So, of course, she scuffed, stumped, and probably chewed her shoes at the end of every school year. She wanted to leave no doubt as to whether or not a new pair was coming. Amber often expressed to me that she felt her mother loved the older brother more than her.

Her first boyfriend was a much older man who bought her a few outfits, and gave her lunch money to go off campus to eat. At our high school, going off campus to get your lunch was a huge status symbol. She commented how good it felt to have someone truly care for you. Upon graduating, she went away to school. Her relationship became estranged due to the long distance. She dropped out of school to come back home to patch up the relationship. To Amber, he was the only person who had ever shown he loved her.

She came home and worked various jobs just to be near the love of her life, according to her. A love built on some cheap trinkets. Amber excused his cheating and frequently bad treatment of her as "not a big deal." Her dream of becoming a schoolteacher was discarded, because she spent the bulk of her time working to keep the only person that (in her mind) had ever loved her.

Years later, the two of them got married and had a son together. I felt happy that she was happy with her decision. Hopefully, now she could let go of childhood demons that were constantly affecting her adult decisions.

I visited her two weeks after her son's sixth birthday. We did the chitchat about our lives like women commonly do. I played with her adorable son in a room filled with toys as she prepared lunch for us all. Just as I was saying my goodbyes, she called me into her laundry room. There was a washer and dryer but the entire room was filled with unopened toys. She told me her son gets everything she can think to give him and she doesn't care that he doesn't play with most of it. Fifteen years later, her childhood beliefs were still controlling her focus.

Numerous adults spend years of their short lives trying to get over events from their childhood. Negative parental experiences can lead to feelings of unworthiness. You may become trapped in a cycle of "proving your worth." Working to make up for deficiencies your parents probably unconsciously placed in your head. Instead of working to fulfill your life's purpose, which is to ultimately "become your potential," you may go through life attempting to gain whatever you lacked as a child. This can be love, security, validation, or even self-esteem.

You can become quite similar to a "chicken chasing its own shadow." The chicken catches a glimpse of her shadow and goes in an endless circle after it. She will wear herself out running after that shadow. Only to end up in the spot from which she began breathless and exhausted. Yet the moment she sees her shadow once again, the race is on. This is not a judgment on how your parents raised you. All of us parents are simply doing the best we can with what we have. There is no book of instructions included with kids when they are born into our lives. Usually parents raise their children the way their parents raised them. Each generation utilizes habits and patterns from the past, regardless of whether they are good or bad. The greatest realization is that you have the power to change what no longer serves you, and retain what does.

Habits and patterns dictate where we focus the majority of our energy. This is why we must replace negative habits and patterns with positive. Our lives, good or bad, are born out of the areas on which we focus most. This awareness is an outstanding advantage when properly utilized. Whatever you like in your life, keep, and whatever no longer serves you, decide to throw it away, right now. You will need two sheets of paper to complete this quick exercise.

Make a list of all your good choices on one sheet of paper, and next make a list of choices you are less than proud of on the other sheet. Next, look at each of your poor choices, ball the paper up, and toss it in the garbage. Look at your good choices, and make the decision to build off of these. The best decisions are meaningless without concentrated focus. Use the strength of your confidence in making good choices to act on your present decisions. I believe in a good philosophy when seeking positive change. You need to expand on your positive qualities to accomplish meaningful goals. When you build on top of strengths, you won't have to make up for your weaknesses.

Some advocate using the fear of negative consequences to encourage more positive actions. This does work for a lot of people, because of a lack mentality. Some fear lost more than they are motivated by gain. However, many will achieve limited results with this method of thinking because a negative focus depletes energy needed to attain your goal. Most of us will only beat ourselves up over decisions we made in an unchangeable past. You become stuck in the same pointless pattern of expanding on traits that no longer serve you. This technique usually creates a negative feedback loop: "I have made bad choices in the past, therefore I will make negative choices in the future." Living the best life means raising your present expectations to a point where only the best life has to offer will do. You will require impenetrable focus to raise your expectations. Gain the ability to concentrate your focus by removing belief structures that are no longer relevant. Next, develop a positive feedback loop to stimulate positive actions.

During a particularly difficult situation, a friend offered this advice, "When life gives you lemons, make lemonade."

My response? "I'm going to make a punch, and forget about the lemons altogether."

I have never liked the "When life gives you lemons, make lemonade" quote. Basically, this quote is saying to do the best you can with bad circumstances. Even with adding water and sugar, the lemons are still the star of the show. What about minimizing the lemons to just one of several ingredients? In a real life example, the lemons would become a call to action, signaling to you that now is the time to make something new and better….an outstanding alternative to making a bad circumstance a little less bad.

Stop allowing life's circumstances to dictate to you, and start dictating to life your circumstances. Now that you expect only the best outcomes for yourself, it is easy to decide to overcome any circumstance that is presently affecting you, regardless of what the circumstances are. Right now you're thinking, yeah, this is easier said than done. It may be difficult to absorb this psychology when you are wondering how you are going to eat. Will you find a job that will pay your bills? Will my intimate relationship survive? There are always going to be ups and downs in life, hence the phrase "life's uncertainties." Don't allow your current circumstances to cheat you out of living your best life. There is no circumstance that can take away mental free will. Decide right this minute that you are going to control the direction of your life.

I would never say motivating yourself in the midst of adversity is as simple as a snap of the fingers. On the contrary, this is going to be some challenging work with terrific results. You are going to create the circumstances you want. Hard work should not deter you from making changes in your life. Your life, your responsibility, no one can make changes except you, and that's a good thing. Why on earth would anyone want someone else to make decisions for him or her?

Answer this question: Which of your parents' pieces of advice usually sticks with you? Something they advised you against that you haven't directly or indirectly experienced or something that they advised you against that you did? For example, your parents tell you to eat a lot of fruits and vegetable to maintain a healthy weight. You know for a fact that what they are saying is true, yet you're model thin and eat like a horse. So, you never really believe their advice. Now, fast forward a few years later, you are twenty pounds above your personal ideal weight. You are going to say, "My parents told me so," but only because you have had a personal experience, which goes back to you deciding to decide. Their advice did not become meaningful to you until you decided it was meaningful information.

Some waste their days thinking about everything they can't do, I spend my days acting on everything I can.

From the Mouth of Babes

One of my younger brothers had absolutely no patience. He would cry hysterically if he didn't get his way with, well, everything. We would be in the middle of the supermarket buying groceries on our four to five times a week visits (yes, Mother went to the store a lot) and Terrence wanted toys, food, tooth picks, and all things in between. The worst part was that he had an eardrum piercing scream that could drive you crazy. Our mother would attempt to appease him using one method only, "Just wait Terrence, I will get it later." Now, later could mean a few minutes, a few weeks, or never. Her objective in these moments was to stop the tantrum with promises of delayed happiness. I, being a little girl, would think to myself, "Well, he's just going to want something new when he does get it." I knew something as a child that I had to relearn as an adult. Thinking you will be happy when a specific event takes place or you get a new toy in some distant or not so distant future is "pure madness."

Let's be honest here. We all have a version of the "rescue fantasy" playing in our brains. I will be happy when BLANK happens. Blank can be a promotion, a relationship, going to school, etc. These hopes of delayed happiness can make you crazy, much like my brother's piercing screams. To start, the promise of future joy is going to let you down. Whatever you are hedging your bet of happiness on is going to be disappointing, even when exactly what you wanted to happen happens. Notice I didn't say if the "thing" happens, because we usually get much of what we anticipate in one way or another.

The problem is there are infinite needs to be met in our lives, and if you never have enough you will never get more. These two simultaneous realities make it virtually impossible to be happy with this mentality. You can't get from outside what is only available to you on the inside. Therefore getting what we want often becomes anti-climactic. We get what we want, and we're still so unhappy. What a surprise! My brother was never satisfied either, because he always had some new absolute "must have." That is the problem with placing your happiness on conditions outside of you. The best conditions cannot rescue you from you, pure and simple. Your thinking is blocking your awaiting joy. Our brains are designed to soothe our ailments. Sometimes, when individuals have a tragic event take place they are unable to remember the details. Their minds block the event out because of the pain it may cause, which is good. That being said, the delusion of delayed happiness is not in itself a tragic event. The amount of time you remain in limbo waiting, though, can become the tragedy of an unfulfilled life.

Our brains seek to protect us from a certain underlying truth lurking in the dark corners of our minds, that little voice that whispers, "Maybe I'm just unhappy." A friend of mine once said to me, in a huffy voice, "You're bored because you are boring." She had the right to comment, because I repeatedly complained of being bored in her company. That was a huge slap in the face to her, because I was being unknowingly insulting. Her statement was packed with a great truth even if she was lashing out because of annoyance. How does that saying go, "Don't shoot the messenger?" Our feelings, and in this case our happiness, are our responsibilities. We are unhappy because we are allowing circumstances to dictate to us, instead of dictating to circumstances. Or we may be entertaining unhappy thoughts – remember the "You're bored because you're boring" statement.

This alone is responsible for a number of people feeling positively overwhelmed by their existence. They buy into the commonly held practice of "have more to be more." Anyone who pursues a goal with the sole hope of being happy once the goal is completed is utilizing a "have more to be more" approach. Have more to be more is the belief in the next big thing. You believe that if you get this big thing, you're headed in the right direction, but you're actually drifting further away. Happiness is not a tangible object to be acquired. You must derive happiness from your actions and not just the results. Living for results will drain your energy to persevere. We must cultivate an environment of happiness within ourselves. You must first breed the emotion of happiness in your brain prior to any actions. Living for the joy of "goal accomplished" will wear you out both physically and mentally. Only those who put into practice a daily habit of being happy repeatedly make it to the achievement finish line.

One cultivates an environment of happiness through being grateful today for the countless opportunities of today. You have to be happy with exactly where you are this moment, and know you are indeed a whole person right now. This type of person will be happy in the present and optimistic regarding the future. They will not cower in a proverbial corner desperately waiting for a rescue from "I'll be happy when….." Their "when" is every day they are blessed to awaken still here on earth. Most of the suffering in this life is caused by wanting something to be different this instant. We sit around thinking about the things we would do if A,B,C,D magically changed overnight. A "magical" change, however, would do us a grand harm. We would be robbed of the joy that comes with conquering adversity. "Adversity does not build character it reveals it," said James Lane Allen. The true prize is the new improved character qualities you will unveil on your journey. Only the journey can make the prize worthwhile, because otherwise the award is empty.

I can remember sitting in a large arena waiting to receive my college diploma. My mind immediately ran to the thought that I was the first in my family to graduate high school, and now a university. I thought about how I had shown with action, not words, how wrong those people were who doubted my ability to follow through because I had become a teenage mother. I thought about my sometimes hour walk to school in hundred degree heat when I didn't have money to ride the bus. I also thought of numerous opportunities I could now give my young son. These thoughts made the degree I received priceless.

A bed made of broken glass gets comfortable if you lie down on it long enough.

Beliefs Habits Patterns

Beliefs lead to the unconscious habits of living that create our lives. Thousands of people wake up every day feeling absolutely trapped. They desperately want to break through to a happier, more fulfilled state. Yet, they never realize they are locked into a life map they drew, and can therefore redraw. These people think there is no way out of their current conditions, or that the way out is too hard to achieve.

An elderly aunt of mine had a saying: "You can only pick what you grow. You planted peas, and want to pick carrots." She would say this anytime someone in the family complained of not getting what they wanted. For years, I had absolutely no idea what point she was trying to convey. Why would a person plant one vegetable and expect to get another type? But that's exactly what a lot of us do every day, in one way or another. Anytime your expectations consistently differ from your actual results, you are planting the seed of a belief that can later prove unhelpful to your growth. This cliché is built on the same principle of "You reap what you sow."

~ CHAPTER 11 ~
The Road to Nowhere is Paved with the Best of Intentions

An important self-development principle is to have a crystal clear vision of exactly what you want and why. Many use a vision board as a physical symbol of what they would like to attract. Some have to figure out their particular purpose. Others know their heart's deepest desire, and still miss the mark. The clear picture of what you want needs to be in your mind in vivid detail. You come up with a plan to live within your purpose, begin to walk in the right direction, and get lost. This happens because somewhere on the path you lose sight of your destination. You become distracted by some shiny object, and forget why you are there in the first place.

I grew up with Kevin. He is the smartest person I've ever met. We all have that one person that is quick in everything. This guy didn't study for college physics and still received A's without blinking one eye. Unfortunately, self-awareness has nothing to do with intelligence level. You can be an Einstein runner up, and be totally unaware of how lost you are.

Kevin has been working somewhere since he became old enough to work. He said part of being a man meant having money in your pocket. First, he worked for a couple of years as a part-time bagger in a local grocery. Next, he got a job that he was excited to land working as a valet in a nice hotel. What man wouldn't want to drive expensive cars eight hours a day, and get paid for the privilege?

He truly enjoyed working there the first few months when his excitement about driving expensive cars was still high. He was hired during the hotel's slow season so the tips weren't great. Not to mention, the valets were required to pool their tips. In other words, all tips were to be placed in one box. At the end of the night, the tips are split between the coworkers. It's an okay system if everyone plays by the rules, but that wasn't the case. Hotel guests gave the tips directly to the valet. He would then, ideally, place the tip in the common box, but some tips never completed their journey to the box. Therefore, he earned very little money in the busy season when there were a lot more cars to park.

Kevin did like the idea of being paid most of his money in tips, because he had become accustomed to going home with cash in his pocket after a day of work. Having to rely on others to be honest was the one downside. So, he began applying for doorman jobs where he could keep his tips. Hotel experience gave him a foot in the door to just about any hospitality position. He was immediately hired as a doorman for one of the most expensive hotels downtown. The tips were very good, some days he would leave work with three hundred dollars in his pocket. Not bad for opening a few doors or carrying a bag or two, right?

On the surface, Kevin had a nearly perfect employment situation. There was just one little problem. His career plan was to become an engineer. Remember, he got A's in college physics without studying for tests. Kevin said that as a child he was constantly interested in how machines worked. He would take apart his parent's radio just to see how the components worked together. Kevin's dad would spank him for what he perceived to be a destructive habit. Kevin laughed and said, "The next day I would take a clock apart." Later he taught himself how to put the electronics back together so he couldn't be punished for his natural curiosity. Kevin told me, "I knew back then what I wanted to do as a career." Now, his dream part-time job conflicted with his future career.

A hotel can have several valets on one shift. Being a doorman, though, was more a one man job. This makes the working hours unpredictable. Kevin had zero choice when it came to hours he could work. His grades began to suffer, and he reluctantly took a break from school. He forgot his goal was to find a job to fit his school schedule, not fit school around a job. The plan was to find a job that would keep money in his pocket and then go back to school. Kevin was painting himself into a corner with his own paintbrush.

He said he searched for other types of jobs. In the end, however, he would just have a doorman job at a new hotel. Kevin would claim that the new job provided more schedule flexibility, which never turned out to be the case. He returned to school a few times, and would withdraw prior to the end of the semester or only barely pass his courses. He said hotels were the only places he could easily find a job because of his experience.

Kevin lost sight of his goal because he became distracted by living life. Most of us fail to see just how day-to-day activities can throw you terribly off course. Thousands of people fall into whatever is nearest, and later dig their holes deeper with paper-thin justifications. It's easy to look at Kevin and think, "He had no excuse because of XYZ." The lesson here is that no one has an excuse not to experience the greatest life ever. Kids, work, spouses, and all the other millions of commitments we have are conditions we must work around. You the person are in full control of what you decide to do. There isn't a single situation in the entire universe where a person hasn't persevered and made their way out.

A Consciousness is Priceless

Haiti is currently the poorest country in the Western Hemisphere. The majority of people in Haiti live on approximately two dollars a day. Few have running water or access to a clean water source. Alternatively, they find the nearest pond. They live in one-room huts with dirt floors and scarce personal possessions. Schools there are privatized, which means getting an education is largely out of reach for many Haitian children. Thousands of Haitians eat a single meal daily if they are lucky. Therefore, there isn't any money left over to pay for school. In Haiti, wealth is controlled by a small elite class. People born at the bottom stay on the bottom, and those born on top stay on top.

Stories of poor Americans aspiring to a wealthy status is quite common. These stories are timeless, because it happens in every time period and regardless of economic conditions. America is truly the land of continuous opportunity. One needs only to have a clear vision, determination, and unwavering faith to accomplish their dream. Becoming a millionaire in the United States isn't easy, but it is clearly possible. Millions around the world envy our opportunities.

Now, imagine being born an impoverished Haitian with no promise of a better tomorrow. You have no inspiring stories of a person just like you living their greatest desires. On the contrary, statistics show you will probably be poorer than your parents. Becoming a self-made millionaire seems virtually impossible in your country, especially for someone like you. You are a dark skinned man with no wealthy background or high status on which to rely.

Well, for a man named Mathias Pierre being born without a silver spoon would not determine his faith. He refused to allow his conditions dictate his life possibilities. As a young man, he read the book *Think and Grow Rich* and used what he learned. He wanted to own a modern computer store similar to stores in the United States. Mathias kept his positive thoughts in the forefront, and obtained one of the few scholarships offered to disadvantaged students. Mr. Pierre changed his consciousness from one of scarcity to abundance. He used his brainpower, combined with consistent action, to "Think and Grow Rich" even with no previous examples for inspiration.

Our lives are created by thoughts, whether positive or negative. Thoughts care nothing about present conditions. Consistently held thoughts are things that show up as the lives we live. Your thoughts will, without fail, deliver your reality. If you truly desire to change your life in a significant way, change the way you think.

Successful Living is for the Few

There is a prevailing mindset in our culture that true success is for the few. Keep in mind successful people are those who live within their purpose. They wake up excited to be alive, ready to experience all the joys life has to offer. These people know life isn't perfect and therefore don't expect perfection. They do expect the numerous opportunities life brings each moment we are blessed to take a breath. Every day we wake up with a choice to enjoy our day, or chose the alternative. Successful people chose to enjoy.

Thousands of people believe that being dissatisfied is an acceptable form of living. They stomp through their existence with heavy feet. These mentally stuck human beings dream up better circumstances in their minds, and never make one attempt to bring their thoughts into the real world. Further, they complain that to do so would be too hard or probably wouldn't work. We reinforce our negative views with information received from our outside world.

Take a quick glance at the numerous negative inputs we receive on a daily basis, and this state of mind is completely understandable. Ninety percent of the local news is covering something bad in the economy, recent murders, or various types of random violence. Let's not even begin to discuss the daily newspaper or national news. Our personal conversations are filled with complaints regarding employment, intimate relationships, or the human condition. Random tidbits of information enter our brains randomly without an invitation. We are being mentally influenced by whatever happens to cross our paths, which is usually negative.

We fall into a habit of thinking, feeling, and acting as if life is an unfortunate jail sentence that we must endure. Many of us seldom realize our entire living experience is solely controlled by our individual thoughts. So we focus on ways to best survive our plight, instead of how to thrive in life. We want to cover and duck all the "what if the worst happens." We think that anticipating the worst somehow cushions the blow. Or we merely fall into a negative habit of imagining the worst possible outcomes. In truth, much of what we worry about either never happens, or even when it does, anticipating it doesn't make you feel any better.

We tell ourselves lies about "successful living" that hold our hands in the short term, and leave us cold in the long. No one wants to face the potentially game-changing truth: Your life is your responsibility to mold into "exactly what you want." Successful people learn to never complain about current circumstances that exist in their lives. They go out into the world and create the circumstances they want. Successful living is available to everyone who seeks it. Most, however, simply allow the influences of their current position in life to block their view.

~ CHAPTER 12 ~
The Good Dog

I have always loved all types of "little" dogs and would constantly beg my mom for a puppy. She would stare at me with the "It's never going to happen," gaze at me, and calmly say, "I don't do pets." In her defense, she was terribly afraid of all animals ever since her kitten incident when she was two years old. She accidently killed her first and only pet. Being a very creative young lady, I decided to quietly begin adopting neighborhood dogs. Of course the true owners were completely unaware of my unofficial adoptions.

Basically, I would hang around friends of mine with dogs especially puppies, and offer to be their personal helper. Dogs, like people, have their own special personalities and idiosyncrasies. Some are obedient and easily trained. Others are somewhat rough around the edges, which in my opinion made those the most interesting.

A particular favorite of mine was a mixed breed by the name of Lil George. His name had to be Lil George because Shelita's dad was Big George. Shelita lived down the street, and her close proximity made it easy for me to visit "my puppy" often. Lil George was a wild extremely excited animal that licked everyone he met. Shelita and her parents tried, without success, to train Lil George to behave properly. They wanted him to sit when told, come when called, and learn to be their idea of a well-trained pet. Personally, I loved Lil George exactly the way he was created.

It is important that a dog is appropriately trained if he is to become a real member of the family. Trained animals can be taken more places with their owners. A short walk to the park became a full-blown networking session for Lil George. He would spontaneously attempt to lick every park visitor that crossed his path. Still, his desire to "be himself" quickly turned him into my favorite adopted pet. Different is usually much more interesting than the same any day of the week, in my book. Lil George had a sparkle in his eyes that wasn't present in my other "well-trained pets."

"You were born an original. Don't die a copy." ~ John Mason

We are all born with that same sparkle of endless possibilities in our eyes. Babies and young children are the most inquisitive. We all start off the same way, looking around at our brand new world and seeing everything we can do. Later, most of us will be taught for the rest of our lives what we can't do. This creates an innate fear of failure, so that we fear attempting all things that fall outside of our learned comfort zone.

Our parents, teachers and those closest meant us no harm. They only wanted to protect us from scrapes, falls, and disappointments. They did for us the same as their loving parents had done, with the best of intentions, for them, believing life is much easier when you learn to "sit" when commanded and walk down a well-traveled road, thinking the secured existence is found within the fence rather than outside in open space – never realizing that living a secure life is more an ideal than a reality.

Let's be perfectly clear. I believe people should commit themselves to a lifetime of education. There is no growth in the human experience without a devotion to learning. First, uncover what it is you would like to do. Then and only then can you figure out what type of education you will require. There are businesses and careers that ask for no more than a commitment from you to do what is required. Be aware, though, that every endeavor will involve you consistently improving your skill set.

Some professions will require your attendance at college or technical school. Go to school and get the education that you need to push ahead. Many allow their present situation to turn into permanent stagnation, where they end up sitting in one spot. Complaining to everyone within earshot about why they are unable to accomplish their goals. You also have what I refer to as the "I'm gonnas." These people make plans that remain plans. They rarely act upon any of their well-designed life plans. These individuals are simply waiting for the perfect moment to start. The only problem with this theory is that the perfect time does not exist because there is always "something" going on in our lives. There just isn't enough money or time or "something" to do what you really want to do.

The fastest way to pull yourself out of this mindset is to decide to begin where you are right now. Your life is happening this very moment. We should act and develop plans that begin with this current moment. For the longest time, I would feel extremely excited each time I wrote down a plan to accomplish a particular goal. The plan would begin with "I will do blah" and "I will achieve blah." The plans, however, would leave out exactly what I was going to do that very moment. Consequently, there was this gap between the plan and acting on the plan.

~ CHAPTER 13 ~
The Power of Choice

Clarity and Goals

To define clear goals you must Ask, Receive, and Move.

There is no permission needed. Invest in yourself. Stop asking for permission to do what you want to do. Be patient. Stop being attached to the outcome.

Goal Attainment Process

1. Clarity
2. Actionable Plan
3. Persistence

Actual goal attainment is a process that begins with clarity. You have to know where you want to go. How else could you know when you got there? There is absolutely no way of getting around the need to be clear. This means stating your goal in specific language, such that there is no doubt what the result should look like. For example, if your goal is to stop drinking alcohol five months from this day, in five months you will either be drinking or you won't. It's that simple. Here's the opposite of clear: I want to drink less. How do you measure what is less to know if you are on track? Less can be five bottles of beer a day instead of six. You may want to go down to one beer a day, you may want to only drink on weekends, or you may want to stop altogether. There is no way to measure if you have accomplished your goal without clarity.

Finding clarity is like looking for a needle in a haystack with a flashlight – even if it's there you probably won't find it.

There is one major problem with looking for clarity: the looking part. Searching for clarity implies that it is lost, sitting on the side of some untraveled road hoping for you to drive by and scoop clarity up before someone else does. Real clarity, born out of what you value, is permanently positioned inside of you. Our daily thinking is what has gotten lost. Your thinking is lost in a sea of 'ought to', 'need to', and 'should do.' It's lost in irrelevant gossip with your friends and information in the media that has nothing to do with you. Who cares whether or not Katie Holmes and Tom Cruise are having another baby? Who cares which new reality star is doing what with whom? This information has no impact on your personal life. This cloudy brain function covers our clarity from view like an impenetrable cloak. I thought, like a lot of the population, that clarity is something that you must find. This way of thinking is an example of the "outside in" approach to life. The basic principle is that happiness or being in joy comes from the outside. In other words, your external accomplishments create your internal happiness. In reality, your outside life must be an external expression of your inside truth for sustainable happiness and value-driven clarity.

The thought that you can find clarity somewhere outside of you really makes no sense. Yet, at some point we all fall into this failed thought pattern. The big secret reason why? Because all the cool kids around town are doing it. We have all been taught by adults all over the place to "do this to get that." You go to college or choose a particular profession to have better opportunities to make more money. So you can then "find" your very own piece of the happiness cake. We have all heard those surrounding us use the terms "find happiness" or "you get happiness by doing blah blah." A lot of self-development practitioners talk about finding clarity. They advise the use of meditation to find your clarity or specific purpose. I believe whole-heartedly that meditation or undisturbed quiet will uncover the path that awaits you. But that's all it does, is uncover the path. I believe that the act of searching for what is not lost takes you away from clarity. Searching takes you outside of yourself instead of looking within.

Begin with Clarity

First absorb that you are already in possession of clarity regardless of what you are telling yourself. Clarity is a reconnection to your inner truth, you are saying hello to what is real. You may presently be burying your clarity beneath self-defeating activities. Your thoughts of doubt, fear, and disappointment are more persuasive than a millionaire offering a blank check. The persuasive commentary in your head is not necessarily true or helpful. Think about it. Our brain will remind us of something we have forgotten at the store on the drive home. That information would have helped inside the store. Now, that same information becomes another source of annoyance. How about when your brain whispers that you aren't good enough for that great job, or a big promotion. Even with your extensive experience in the field? Secondly, you may be confusing lack of clarity with refusing to take deliberate action. I assert that we are quite clear in numerous areas of our lives. It may simply be more comfortable to latch on to being unclear. Foggy clarity provides you with an excuse to not take deliberate action, because action is risky. Things may turn out differently from how you pictured it would. A known hell is much more comfortable than an unknown paradise to masses.

This is why it is important to distinguish between clarity and failure to take deliberate action. Imagine someone is in an intimate relationship with someone that's completely wrong for them. You know Mr. or Mrs. Not-the-One is wrong because they tell you constantly. If this is you, then you won't have to do a bunch of work imagining. If you had a penny for every time they complained about how awful he or she is, you would be a millionaire. Their list of complaints never decreases, only grows with the passing of time. They claim to want nothing more than to leave this dead-end relationship. They are unclear as how to get out of the relationship. Yet if you even suggest leaving, they can and will provide a laundry list within seconds as to why they can't (won't) end it without horrible consequences. They may use excuses like kids, money, or wanting to avoid divorce. This person claims they need only to be shown a way out and without pause would be out the door.

This is not a lack of clarity, this is a refusal to take action. Yes, kids, money, wanting to avoid divorce are real considerations. There is no consideration in the world, however, that should imprison you in a cell of misery. Mr. or Mrs. Want Out is perfectly clear on the condition of their relationship, and the solution. They simply wish there was a way to get what they want without taking any new actions. That was indeed an easy example of refusing to take action.

Here's one that may be a little tougher to swallow in a single gulp. What about the person who stays in a job that they hate, because they have convinced themselves there are no other realistic options? Our options and opportunities are limitless. It's usually our thoughts that are limited.

What about those that pretend to be utterly confused as to what direction to walk, out of fear? They fear that what they want is less than their idea of realistic. Take the person that claims to have no idea what to do next with their life. Ask this person, "What would you do if you were free to do whatever you wanted to do?" Tell them they have enough money to never worry about a bill ever again. Their time is their own to do as they wish, and only as they wish. Yes, at first they will begin to say what many say. "I would take a trip around the world to experience foreign cultures." "I would buy a mansion, ten cars, etc." Material items come first to us all, because we have an "outside" in approach to our lives.

Once they get all that out of their system, repeat your question a bit more slowly "What would you do if you were free?" There is literally a magical component to the word free, because freedom is abstract. Feeling free is a solely individual experience, being free has different meanings for different people. You may want to be free of bills, your friend may want to be free of a toxic relationship, and your parents may want the freedom to sail around the world. That's why in this exercise, one's true values begin to trickle out like a slow dripping faucet. Remember, many of us have not considered our true life's direction in years, or quite possibly never.

It would be unreasonable to expect that complete clarity is going to pour out of you on the first turn of the knob. Your clarity will show itself in spots, like clear water coming out of a rusty pipe. There seems to be all rusty water flowing at first. Within a minute or two the water is obviously clearer, and if the water is allowed to continue running it will become crystal clear. This is exactly the process to connecting to your innate clarity. Your clarity, like the clear water in the pipe, is always there. You just have to clear out the rust.

Be Clear on Getting Clear

Now that you know that clarity is a stone that you already hold in your hand, decide to take complete responsibility for your clarity. You take responsibility by making clarity part of your daily routine. That means actively participating in activities that build clear, purpose-directed thinking. One way to accomplish this is by making a short list of what you are clear on. For some this is a fairly easy activity to undertake, because we all have parts of our lives that we really enjoy. For example, you may be very happy with your friendships. You know these people are in your corner through thick and thin, and you are thankful. You may be happy with your current employment because you have found work that you enjoy with advancement opportunities. Use what you are clear on to feed your feelings of certainty. It is easier to build a house that already has a strong foundation. You are merely adding layers to what is already standing on solid ground. On the other hand, a house with no foundation has to be developed from the ground up with nothing to nail your boards to. When you build up what's strong, you never have to make up for what's weak.

Some are still saying while reading this, I have no idea what I want to do with <u>fill in the blank</u>. Therefore I am unable to be clear in regards to my next step. You're thinking, I cannot build on top of what isn't there in the first place. You are clear about what you don't like in your life right now, because the negative is always visible. For me, I was tired of being held back from living a life created out of my divine purpose. My fear of failure, the opinions of others, change, my story, self-sabotaging thoughts and going against the status quo were all wringing the light out of me. It's nearly impossible to locate what matters when you are whole-heartedly invested in what doesn't. I turned my "don't wants" into their opposites to create positive clarity. I didn't want to live the life that others in my close circle thought was "realistic." I did the opposite. I concentrated on living the life that was realistic for me. Today, am I always sure as to what direction I should travel? No, but I do usually get to where I need to be much faster than in the past. You must begin with what you have, even if you have no idea what you want to do. Decide to be clear that you are, right now, discovering what you want to do. You are never lost, only exploring your infinite opportunities to find the right fit.

In your heart, you know that everything you will ever need to be successful in any area of your life is already present within you. This is how you have gotten all the successes in your life to this point. Think back to times that you have been crystal clear on where you were going. You simply knew within your being that you were going in the right direction. Sure, you may have justified your choices with "I'm really good at this," "I have the necessary training," "I'm really getting great experience," or "We have a lot in common." In reality, our choices at the time felt like the right thing to do on the inside. You may have been focusing your attention on confusion, which is the opposite of clarity. This is why you believe that clarity is a foreign language you have to be taught. We practice the opposite of clarity each time we use words like lost, afraid, confused, or phrases such as "don't know which way to turn" and "wish I knew." These practices beat down on our inner strength, which leads to feelings of weakness that serve to multiply our self-doubt.

Hold On to Your Clarity Like a Dog to A Bone

Clarity is an exercise of choice. You either choose to be clear or you, by default, choose confusion. Remember you always possess clarity because it resides within you. It gets covered in our self-sabotaging habits. Once you consciously choose clarity by removing the baggage currently hiding it from view, you must hold on to it with the grip of a hungry dog on a fresh juicy bone. The same factors that hid your clarity are lurking right around the corner: the fuzzy-headed friends filled with their personal doubts and confusion, the well-meaning naysayers that only want to protect you from what they perceive as inevitable disappointment, the potential for a disorganized life is forever present created by reacting to the fires of the day. Or, we allow the needs of others to outweigh the needs of ourselves. Throw in what you never saw coming, like job loss, divorce, illness, or death of a loved one, and you have countless factors that could nudge you into confusion.

You must have tunnel-vision focus when it comes to maintaining your level of clarity. A perfect example that comes to mind is the way Dorothy in the *Wizard of Oz* stuck to her desire to go home. She was unhappy with her life until she realized there was no place like it. Once she absorbed this fact, she was determined to get back there. Regardless of what she encountered on her journey down the yellow brick road, she was focused on getting to the Emerald City to meet the wizard. Dorothy was told he was the one that could give her what she wanted most, which was to get home to Kansas. On this road she meets both friends and obstacles that threaten the success of her journey. Still, Dorothy is crystal clear that she wants to be home again. Her outside reality has no bearing on Dorothy's level of inner clarity.

What's going on outside should have no impact on your level of clarity. I am not encouraging you to ignore what has to be addressed in your life. Take care of what needs to be taken care of, just keep your clarity in plain view during the process. What's going in your life right now is what's going on. Events have as much power as we give them. To prove this point, there are people that actually miss the hard times they have triumphed through. The thing they really miss is how perfectly clear they felt during these times. Similar to just about everything in the human experience, how adversity affects you is subjective.

Some people respond like my three-year-old daughter. When the little lady becomes sad for one reason or another, she hits her older brother. I asked her why once, and she looked me right in the eye and said, "I don't know Mama, when I get sad, things get fuzzy." I am comparing the "things get fuzzy" part of the statement, so disregard the hitting. For others, adversity creates a clarity unlike they have ever known before. The clarity about the goal they are pursuing most likely becomes their anchor during the turbulence.

Our circumstances can cloud our thoughts, creating uncertainty and confusion. That's why once you uncover your clarity you must hold on to those thoughts and feelings until the habit sticks. Many of us have developed the habit of uncertainty and confusion. We think of clarity as an infrequent, but welcome visitor always ready to flee. Therefore, the idea of clarity as a natural state of existence seems impossible. Remember, even when you are unsure of what direction to walk in, you are never lost. You are simply exploring your options. Thoughts of being lost speak to confusion, which creates the opposite of clarity. Making a habit of clarity can be a challenge, though it is completely doable with a little practice.

Once you make the choice to be clear on what you want, then it will be time to create goals you are determined to attain.

Clarify Your Goal: Don't Know is as Don't Know Does

As stated earlier, the first step in accomplishing what you want in every endeavor is being clear on exactly what you do want. The best way I've found to do this is by writing down your goal on a sheet of paper. If you are in the middle of a restaurant when the idea hits you, write it on a napkin. No napkin available at the time? Type it on your phone. The point is, if you haven't absorbed it already, is to get your goal down somewhere. Otherwise your all-important goal becomes at best a "wish" and at worst "a fleeting thought." Writing down your goal provides a solid focus point.

When your goal is left hanging in the air, it's easy for it to drift and ultimately get lost. Writing or declaring your goal is a form of manifestation. Dictionary.com defines the word Manifest as, "Readily perceived by the eye or the understanding; evident; obvious; apparent; plain." Your goal needs to be evident to you at all times. That way, you will work on those activities that lead you to accomplishing your goal. The quickest route between any two points is a straight line. This is true when doing geometry, and this is true in life. A goal that is written somewhere you will frequently see it becomes plain, self-evident. So you literally walk in a straight line to exactly what you are seeking. Having a clearly stated goal keeps you focused, regardless of what's going on around you.

Once You Are Clear

Clarity is an absolute necessity when setting up your very important goal. You have to be clear on what you want to accomplish, if your accomplishments are to bring you real satisfaction. Unearthing your personal clarity gives meaning to your goals. Pursuing the wrong goals is like spending the entire day getting ready for a party and ending up at the wrong house. For the sake of this discussion, let's assume you are crystal clear about one life expanding goal. I'm talking about a goal that would change your life as you know it, today. Jack Canfield refers to these goals as "stretch goals," because they stretch you beyond your usual comfort zone. A stretch goal should get you tingly, excited when visualizing its completion. It's the kind of goal that's going to require actions that make you uncomfortable, as a rule. You expand beyond the current borders of your life when you are uncomfortable. In my opinion, discomfort is where passionate living takes place.

I use the term life-expanding goal not in an attempt to give an old title a new name; I use the term life expanding because of the way it makes me feel. Life expansion creates enthusiasm within my being as I visualize living a bigger, fuller life. A rich life is one dessert you can eat as much as you like, and gain healthy pounds of experience. For me, this is a life where I not only live my deepest truth, but encourage millions to do the same. This goal is crystal clear in my mind, and therefore gets a goal pole. A goal pole is a list of tasks you must carry out before you can reach the flag. The flag is whatever life-expanding goal you have fashioned in your mind.

In the goal pole method, you draw a pole with a flag at the top on a sheet of paper. You can also use a poster board to create a larger goal pole. You can draw hatch marks on the pole spaced by the number of tasks required to reach your goal. Write the goal you are determined to accomplish on the flag first. Next, begin writing whatever tasks must be completed from the bottom up. Your flag should be ordered in a 1st, 2nd, 3rd, etc. system. You can leave space between each main task to write smaller tasks that need to be done.

Another idea is to use pictures that would illustrate each step on your journey to the top of the flag. This method is quite useful if you are a highly visual person that relates to pictures. Say, for example, you wanted to become a hair stylist with your own shop, maybe even have a personal line of products. You could have a picture of someone hard at work studying, a picture of someone styling hair in a salon, a picture of someone looking at real estate to purchase, and a picture of product bottles. For a greater impact, you could even order bottles off the Internet with your product name printed to use in the picture. On the flag there would be a picture of you standing in a salon symbolizing the attainment of your goal.

The method I describe here was adapted from another goal-attaining strategy known as mind mapping. In mind mapping you write your main goal in the middle of a page. Working backwards from your goal, you list what will need to be done to get the goal. You do this by drawing spokes away from the main goal with circles at the end. Inside each circle is the task that needs to be completed. You can draw spokes from those circles listing smaller tasks. I chose to create the goal pole because my mind works in a vertical order. It is important to use the method that works best for your type of thinking. Whether you choose to use paper or poster board, the goal pole needs to be in a place you can constantly view it. When using paper, you can tape it to a bathroom mirror or a plainly visible wall in your house. Another suggestion that I highly recommend, if using paper, is to draw your goal pole in your journal. That way, you will always have access to your goal and you can keep it private from others if you desire privacy.

Create an Actionable Plan

Once you have declared your goal, you can now create your actionable plan. I am not talking about some ten page step-by-step blue print. You want to avoid drowning yourself in an ocean filled with information. This activity is actually counterproductive to getting what you most desire. Often, collecting information convinces us we are earnestly working toward our goals. Often we end up using our information quest as an excuse to stall. Stalling provides fertile ground for our self-limiting fears to grow unchecked. We come up with a million considerations or roadblocks for each new piece of information we gather, leading to one more roadblock in front of what we want to accomplish. We also come up with new considerations that justify why we should wait a little longer to begin. The way we "get" in this life is through "giving" in this life. There is no such thing as a free ride. What you give, which comes in the form of action, is payment.

Information's natural function is to help us decide what actions to take right now. Think about stocks. You want to project how they are going to rise in the future, to purchase them in the now. The now is where life takes place. You can plan forever, but with no consistent action on your side absolutely nothing changes. The collection of information by itself is not an action, no matter how much you attempt to convince yourself. Once you are clear about what you want to do, get enough information to begin now. It is in our present moment that we ever do anything anyway. The future has not been written, and the ink on the past has already dried. It is impossible to be a doctor in the future without going to medical school in the present. This is why doing is more important than knowing exactly what to do. You can always adjust your actions to your new information and experiences.

A Little to the Left

I am a big supporter of the "ready, fire, aim" method to getting ahead. In short, you take a shot at your target, observe where your shot landed, and make the proper adjustments. For example, think about if you were shooting arrows at an apple, Preferably, this would be an apple that is not sitting atop someone's head, for obvious reasons. One clear reason is that you would have a lot more room for error when setting up your shot. Who needs the pressure of someone losing their head, literally? Going back to the example, if your arrow landed too far right of the apple, you would adjust your aim more to the left the next time you took a shot. Similarly, if your arrow landed well above the apple, you would tilt your aim down on your next attempt. Adjusting shots you're taking right now is far more effective than planning the perfect shot to take, and let's face facts, a thousand times more exciting.

I remember attending an event where owners and managers of small businesses were speaking. The purpose of the event was to get a real life look into owning a business. One by one each stepped up to talk about their individual experiences both negative and positive. I remember being completely locked into their speeches. There was one speaker in particular that I keenly remember these several years later. He, by less than coincidence, had used the ready, aim, fire method to solve the obstacles that arose in his business. Of course at the time I had no idea that this method even existed. I was simply attracted to the dancing in the moment approach, instead of waiting to learn the perfect moves. Mr. Beauty Shop, my chosen name for him, was a musician of twenty years turned hair dresser, turned beauty salon owner. How does such a metamorphosis take place, you ask? According to him, he woke up one day and decided he wanted, in his words, work that paid the bills and he wanted to give himself a job.

Upon finishing cosmetology school, he rented a booth to begin his career. He liked the money he was earning, but quickly became unhappy with the rising booth rental fees. So, he decided to open his own shop with himself as the sole employee. The problem he almost immediately encountered happened to be one of the two main reasons he went into business for himself. He found out that opening a business to give yourself a job is a bad idea. The reason is that running a successful business is a lot harder than working a job, and collecting a paycheck. Yes, now he had no rising fees to pay to the shop owner. Now, instead, he was paying rent money to a property owner for his shop space. There was no receptionist to book his appointments. Therefore, he had to answer the phone between working on clients. He, as you can easily imagine, missed possible bookings because often the phone was allowed to ring.

So Mr. Beauty Shop hired a receptionist, and started renting out booths to cover his additional costs as a shop owner. Next, he learned the problem with renting booths from the owner's side of the chair. Yes, pun intended. First of all, many dislike paying part of what they feel is their hard earned money to booth rent. Once they build a large clientele, like Mr. Beauty Shop, they decide to work out of their own space or go somewhere with lower rent. After all, their clients usually feel loyalty to the hairdresser not where the hairdresser does the hair.

At this point, some would have been ready to throw in the towel. Mr. Beauty Shop had addressed each problem that came up, and the problems were still coming. Should he close the shop and go back to renting space? Should he decide to accept the fact that renting booths made his shop that he wanted to grow nothing more than a revolving door? Well Mr. Beauty Shop did neither of the two. He simply adjusted his aim once again. The apple was in plain sight, he was sure to hit if he stayed committed to hitting. Instead of renting booths, he decided to hire beauticians offering them a competitive wage. This way he could break up the services. One cosmetologist would cut your hair while another colored it. The thought being, the customer would then have no personal ties to any one person. Thus Mr. Beauty Shop worried little that a hairdresser would run off with clients. There was also a great benefit for the stylists, according to him. They could rely on a steady check at the end of each week, no more having to hope clients came in to get paid. The practice also allowed stylists to do what they most enjoyed. If your specialty was cutting, you cut; if it was coloring, you colored. Another advantage was that the stylists received bonuses when the salon did well.

This was, for me, positively delicious information to absorb. Here he was, ready, firing, aiming, over and over. Once again, I had no idea that this method existed. I was attracted to his consistent real life action regardless of his immediate outcomes. There was no sitting around planning every detail to the point of immobility. He simply kept firing and adjusting his aim up and down left to right with the goal of hitting the apple.

Persist Until the Universe Can't Resist

Like a really tasty dessert, the last element to the goal attainment process has been left for last. It's important to note that without this element the other two are probably of little value. Persistence is absolutely necessary in getting your goal. The first reason is often you have to be persistent just to get clear on what you want to do. Listening to the noise of the world that comes in the form of outside opinions, negative head chatter, and self-defeating beliefs muffle our true voice. This voice knows at all times what direction we should walk in, because it represents our unfiltered joys and talents. This voice answers to no agenda, only you.

Persistence is a must in clarity because clarity is an everyday exercise, not a onetime event. You must get up each day, and persist in being clear. There are too many ways throughout the day we can become distracted. We commonly mistake prolonged distraction as being confused or needing to make alterations to our plans. In reality, we have simply drifted off course and become frustrated with our lack of progression. Let's say you decide to create a website for an area in which you are legitimately interested. It's important that the example uses a subject of real interest to you, because it is so easy to write off your lack of follow through with, "You know I just wasn't as interested in it as I previously thought." Or take your pick of a million other handy excuses.

For the ladies, let's make the site about proper skin care and for the guys, sports. You're really excited. First, imagining how the site will look, and planning all the elements you will add. You decide to set aside a little time every evening after work to set the website up. This works very well for you for a week, maybe a few weeks. However, the excitement is starting to quickly dwindle, taking your momentum with it. Now you start telling yourself it's too difficult for a regular person to create a website, you do not have enough time, or you tell yourself no one will read it anyway. The truth is, it is a challenge to continue doing anything that takes work once the "great idea" excitement has worn off. It would be lovely if all we had to do was think of something, and the actual work could be handled by someone else.

This is where making the commitment to persist until your goal is accomplished comes into play. You were crystal clear on what you wanted to do, and working your actionable plan. Yet you still fell short of what you wanted to accomplish. To achieve anything in life worth achieving you have to consistently show up. Without persistence you will give up when the going gets rough (and it probably will), regardless of what you choose to do. This includes your brain, because sometimes the rough is completely a mental condition created by what you believe to be possible or not possible. Either way, whether the rough is real or imagined or you just get bored with the process, the commitment to persist until you reach your desired result means you will continue no matter what.

Adapt to the Climate

You have to dance to what's playing

A key component to sustained persistence is the ability to adapt to the present climate. If it were thirty degrees below zero, you wouldn't go outside sporting a bikini. You would put on a coat because it's cold outside. You have to accept whatever is going on in your life, and still move forward in your desired direction.

Some can only move forward when their life is "nice and tidy." We all have that relative or friend whose home could literally be in a magazine. There is a place for everything and everything is in its place. Yet, if you make the grand mistake of forgetting to return one magazine back to its neat stack, you may be arrested and shot at dawn. Everything's perfect as long as the entire environment can be controlled. Don't get me wrong, there's nothing wrong with absolute order. I am a big fan of a "nice and tidy" atmosphere myself. It's just that even without three kids and a husband, absolute order in life is more a sweet old-fashioned notion than reality.

The only element in life you have complete control over is yourself. And if you are similar in any way to millions, you aren't batting 100 in that department. You are doing the best you can with your level of awareness. That's exactly what the entire world does – the best they can with what they have. It is for this reason that the people and circumstances in our lives fall into "the way it is" category. If you want to be successful, these people and circumstances will have to come along for the ride. Truly successful people understand that you must adapt to the climate you have, instead of wasting valuable time wishing things were different.

Think of it like getting all dressed up to go out to a party with your friends. You have purchased a new outfit, had your hair and nails done. You are not one to brag, but you should be on the cover of a magazine. The atmosphere is nice when you arrive at your destination. After three songs, though, you are wondering who is in charge of the music, because you definitely can't dance to what's playing. It's techno and you are rap, it's rap and you're techno, or maybe it's rock and you are roll. Either way the music has got to go. You find out the music was chosen earlier and the selections are playing automatically. There is no way to do anything about what's playing without stopping the music altogether, and that's social suicide.

Now you have a choice to make, you can: A) Decide to go home or B) Decide to stay and dance to what's playing. You look around the room to see what other people are doing, because you can't be the only one that thinks the music is wrong. You notice that many of the party people have left, or look as if they are about to leave. But, there are some that obviously have decided to stay because they are dancing to what's playing. You can tell from their awkward movements this music would not be their first choice either. Yet they have decided to stay and have a good time anyway. They came for a party and they are going to have one.

This is exactly what we must do when it comes to achieving our goals. It would be great if those closest to you were supportive. It would be great if we had a bunch of extra time to get more of what's important to us done. It would be nice if every "I" was dotted and every "T" was crossed in our lives. That's just not the way that life works out, usually. Things get messy, and often the closer you get to what you want, the messier things get. You must develop the ability to adapt to whatever comes up if you are going to sustain your persistence. The events in life, both expected and unexpected, can beat down your momentum. That is why developing your ability to adapt is important to your being continuously persistent.

The Stuff in Between

You see the mountain you wish to climb and walk in its direction, yet the closer you get the further away the mountain becomes.

Self-development is definitely one of those things in life that is, and will continue to be, an ongoing process. I will forever be simultaneously a student and a teacher, which is exactly where I want to be. I bring up this point again here because you can follow the best goal-achievement plan in the world and still fall short of the mark. I speak from personal experience. You can read the books, go to seminars, have outstanding mentors, have the best of intentions, and begin highly motivated, yet your results are not enough to have justified the effort you put forth. There are goals that actually make you feel weaker instead of stronger, because of the stuff "in between." The stuff in between is your thoughts, beliefs, and habits that can ultimately control the direction of your energy.

I am a sucker for those stories where people have dramatic changes occur in their life just by practicing persistence and resilience. You know the stories. From rags to riches, the person appears as if they have no opportunity to overcome, yet through continuous commitment they are able to more than survive, they thrive. For me, it's not about the fame or the money (though of course that's great too). It's more about being shown that you can literally start from where ever you are, and mold your life into exactly what you want it to be. It makes you look at your own struggles and say, "If they can do that with their circumstances, I can surely accomplish my goals." I only want to change careers, go to school, start a business, or find someone with which to spend my life, etc. If you are a mother, you may simply want a clean house. No matter the difficulty of the goal, you still, more often than not, end up disappointed with your results. This has been my situation more times than I would like to admit.

Each time, I hit the invisible wall wondering what the "h-double-hockey-sticks" happened. I read the books, followed the methods, and thought I felt motivated. Yet (and still) at times I'm unable to break the glass to get the prize. I think, "Well, I'm not motivated enough," and so I worked on my personal motivation or said, "I'm not disciplined enough to follow the plan." Yes, these reasons do frequently contribute to poor results, but these are not the sole reasons. You will probably discover, if you haven't already, that these conditions aren't often the main reason why you're falling short of the mark. You are falling short because where you are and where you want to be are in two different countries.

There are goals that you can set that are easy for you to achieve, but would be quite difficult for others and vice versa. The difficulty factor of the goal has little to do with if it gets done or not. It's the "you" factor of the goal that will determine if it gets done.

For example, take two people that decide they want to begin saving their money for the future. Neither person has ever saved any money and they both actually believe, on their limited income, that it isn't even possible. Yet, they both recognize the need to have money saved for their retirement. Their present employers offered no hope of a pension, and they are fearful of, in their words, "sharing space in a cardboard box." They intelligently take their concerns to a financial planner that specializes in helping people with lower incomes so that the advisor is fully educated on how to best help people with their particular circumstances.

Both men are given a plan to reduce expenses to free up cash to be placed in savings. The two are skeptical about the plan. Sir X and Sir Y are concerned about depriving themselves of what they consider to be their small joys. But they agreed to fully commit to the financial action plan. Six months later, Sir Y has successfully saved money, and is happier with life overall. His follow-through has provided him with increased self-assurance. Sir Y was not an extravagant spender to begin with, and found the plan to be a lot easier to fit into his life than he previously thought. He is now looking forward to his financial future instead of turning away in fear.

Sir X's experience, on the other hand, was a completely different story altogether. Sir X was reluctant about the changes at first, but just like Sir Y agreed to implement the financial plan. Six months later, Sir X feels frustrated and disappointed with his results. He found the plan difficult to follow consistently. Cutting back on his spending left him with a feeling of self-imposed deprivation. He thought to himself, "You can't just work to pay bills, you have to treat yourself to something." Still, he desperately wanted the security that savings would provide. So he honestly worked to follow the plan that the advisor had clearly outlined. Yet months later his results didn't match what he believed to be his real effort. Sir X had cut back on a few cash-sucking habits, but not enough to free up any real cash. He had saved some money because that was automatically taken out…. though, because Sir X felt deprived, he had lowered his automatic withdrawals from 20% of his pay to 10% after the second month.

Sir X's self-confidence was lowered, and Sir Y's was higher following the experience.

These two men had the same income, the same financial obligations, and a similar relationship with money. Neither of the two had ever saved. Neither believed they made enough money to even think about saving money. Yet one man achieved his goal and felt encouraged to move ahead further. The other felt disappointed, and probably secretly wished he had never agreed to participate. In hindsight, it's easy to look at the situation and say, "Ummm, he didn't follow the plan that was given to him. That's why he didn't successfully reach his goal." Most people reading this would probably quickly agree with you. Just look at Sir Y's results for the proof.

This is how many people think, and this is also why many of our goals can actually do more harm than good. Sir X and Sir Y's outside circumstances were close, but their internal circumstances were worlds apart. Sir Y was never a spender, he simply thought it was natural to have no money left at the end of a month with what he earned. He had no big money-draining habits to release. He simply spent what he had, because he believed that was his station in life. He frequently thought, "It's a blessing that I have no need for big TV's as thin as a painting on the wall with the money I bring home." He felt pretty confident that if he had the money to save, he would save. Although he was skeptical, he was on board once the financial planner proved he did indeed have the money. He did have places to save, and he could happily live on less. These practices helped him save the money he needed for his retirement.

Now it's pretty easy to say Sir X is lying in the bed he made with his less than ideal choices, case closed. What lurks secretly under his bed covers, however, lurks under the covers of us all in some way. Sir X's actions can only be as effective as his deep-down beliefs. He really wanted to save money, but his beliefs about what was possible for him never received the memo. Sir X may have grown up poor, while being told there's not enough to go around in the world. Maybe this led to a belief that it is impossible for people "like him" to get ahead. The "why" really isn't important, it's all about the end result. Until he aligns himself with beliefs consistent with saving, no financial plan in the world will work.

For you, maybe it's a marriage that you feel you can't leave, for one reason or another. A common reason people use is, "I'm staying so the kids can have both parents." Yes, that is a real factor, but I promise you underneath there is another belief that's keeping you in that marriage. You may be afraid of spending your life alone. You may be afraid of the financial challenge a split from your present spouse would cause. Or, for you, it could be a career or lifestyle for which you can't see your way out. Know that there are thousands of people that have achieved whatever you are working on in a variety of situations. So, we know that the situation can't be the problem. If you have developed plans, mapped out goals, become active, and still aren't really getting to where you want to be, it's probably the stuff in between that is stopping you. For you to get what you want, regardless of the particular goal, you must learn how to first recognize the stuff in between so that you can remove its hold on you, and next learn to properly align your whole self with the goal. That means your mind, body, and soul have to be on the same page.

How to Recognize the Stuff In-Between

Never be afraid of what's lurking around the corner. It's not what's in the dark that gets you, it's what's in the light that you can't see that'll take you down.

Motivation or Happy Panic?

You are not required to use my goal-achievement strategy to get what you want. This strategy works well for me, but there are numerous variations. All variations will have this very basic set up: Decide-Do-Keep Doing. There are goals, however, that won't be achieved regardless of what achievement strategy you use. The reason is that there is stuff on the inside of you that needs to change first. Otherwise you are wasting a bunch of time chasing a wish. I say "wish" instead of "dreams," because you can attain almost anything you dream. It's the wishes that are usually impossible to ever achieve. Wishes are built on a platform of 'no additional work' from you. Basically, you are sitting in a spot wanting a change to occur with no effort from you. It's like saying that you are going to win the lottery someday, yet never even bother to purchase a ticket.

To accomplish anything in this life, you are going to need to be motivated. Motivation touches every aspect of our lives. You have to be motivated to brush your teeth and roll out of bed in the morning. Motivation, in plain terms, is the reason why you do what you do. It is the force that pushes you closer and closer toward your goal. I think of motivation as your goal organizer: it properly aligns your physical, mental, and emotional parts. Motivation guides you to behave in ways that places you on the side of what you want. There are two components of motivation, which are the inside and the outside. The inside component is the most important because it drives you to take physical action toward your goal. Some would describe inside motivation as having the heart or the spirit to win. The outside component is less important than the inside, however, it's still essential to success. The outside should be a mirror image of what's going on inside. Ninety-nine percent of the time, your outside conditions are a matter of perspective, and we know the perspective is an internal creation. Yet if you feel motivated internally, but then convince yourself that external circumstances will not allow you to score even at the goal line, there isn't enough internal motivation in the world that's going to win you the game. You must possess both inside and outside motivation if you are to succeed.

This is why being properly motivated holds such a high position in self-improvement. Because there is such an emphasis on motivation, everyone is quick to jump on the bandwagon. A friend, or maybe even you, will talk about how excited you are to do this and so. You may take some action toward your goal for a while. Yet somehow that goal you were determined to achieve slips into the land of the forgotten. One reason this happens is because what many think is motivation, in reality is "happy panic."

According to Dictionary.com, panic can be defined as "an instance, outbreak, or period of fear." It can be quite easy to mistake fear for determination, especially when you pair the fear with a big dose of what you believe to be positive thinking. Happy panic occurs when you want to accomplish some goal but you are secretly afraid you don't have the "stuff" to get it done. So you pump yourself up with false encouragement. It's false because what you believe deep inside is exactly what you will achieve externally.

This is a bit of a head-scratcher at first read, so give it a minute and I promise the concept will quickly fall into place. We all have instances of allowing procrastination to seep into the important areas of our lives. Or, you might be so cemented into a habit of doing things a certain way that you refuse to pay attention to the clues that "change is a coming." You bury your head in the proverbial sand until you are confronted by an event or personal realization that appears, at least to you, impossible to ignore. Many of us have been conditioned to react, instead of calmly weighing the options, or asking ourselves what we want, and responding appropriately. We start what we truly believe to be goal-focused actions, but it's actually reaction dressed in an ugly wig. One of the ways we react is by developing plans that we don't really believe inside, regardless of how much you want to believe. Remember, authentic motivation requires an internal foundation. Therefore Fear + False-positive Thinking + Reaction= Happy Panic.

In doubt about whether you are experiencing authentic motivation or happy panic? Look at your current results. Are you moving toward your goal day by day, or do you seem to be moving further away? The action plan you developed should set a forward momentum toward your accomplishment. A plan that leads to frustration needs to be readjusted. Realizing that you are in a state of happy panic should be welcomed. You can only control what you can see, and what you are unable to see controls you. Once you know, you can adjust your plan down to goals that you can successfully complete. You can build on these successes to accomplish more.

For example, if your goal is to graduate with a college degree in your field of interest, you could find it difficult to hold down a full-time schedule because of your perceived life situation. You can A) Keep giving yourself pep talks to do better, or B) You can consciously decide to dial down the goal. Plan to take a couple of classes instead of a full-time schedule. I once spoke to a woman who spent nine years getting her Nursing degree. She then immediately went on to get her Masters in less than two years. The last time we spoke, she was actively applying to doctorial programs. I asked, what kept you going through the years? There are a large number of people out there that would have stopped going back. Her response, "A sledge hammer will bring down a wall fast, yet sometimes all you have is a hammer. It'll take a little longer, but the wall still fall." Make a commitment to move forward, if only a little bit. This will keep your eyes focused on results, and keep your eyes off roadblocks.

~ CHAPTER 14 ~

You Will Have to Be New to Do New

To get what you have never had, you are going to have to become someone you've never been.

Maybe it is our culture that makes us all want our desires met right now. There is no time to develop characteristics that will help us grow. I remember when a phone was a phone, a camera was a camera, and you had to watch television on a television. Now you can take a picture, make a call, and watch television from the same device. We want everything in a pre-packaged bundle, preferably with a bow on top. We want what we want without doing much to get it. Yet to get the good stuff in life, some parts of you will have to grow in ways you may have never imagined. Real growth takes time, though how much time is an individual event for each person. I can say this: growth doesn't usually occur overnight for any of us.

To get something new, you are going to have to become new. You can do this by aligning yourself with the energy of what you want. Until you are aligned with what you want, no matter how long you work, I can almost promise real success will continue to escape you no matter how fast you chase it. Whenever I'm driving west in the evening, I imagine myself chasing the sun. I can see the darkness in the rearview mirror. Part of the sun is still right in front of me, yet no matter how fast I drive, I still end up in the dark. Goal attainment without proper alignment is like running after the sun. You may seem close at times, but in the end you will end up in the dark wondering why you can't catch what you can clearly see. You get what you want by controlling the parts of your life that you do indeed control. We have absolute control over what we think, what we do, and what we do about what we think.

There's ads everywhere you look, telling us to be careful of what we eat. There should be just as many telling us to be careful of what we think. Your body is what you eat, but your whole life is what you think.

The Boy Wolf

A fable

Once upon a time, there was a baby boy born to a very poor family. The family lived in what was literally the forest. The mother and father had three children, a pair of ten-year-old twin girls and a newborn son. They did not have an inside bathroom or plumbing with running water of any kind. The entire family went to bed hungry most nights, including the littlest of the bunch. Their home was nothing more than a rambling shack made of mud and sticks. What the family lacked in material items, they made up for in lots of love. For the mother and father were grateful for a family to love.

One day as the family was washing in the nearby creek, as they often did, they placed the baby boy on a couple of nearby logs away from the water. The mother and father were concerned about the baby being too near the water. They made certain that little boy was visible from where the family was washing in the creek. At the same time, a mother wolf was wandering around the forest near the logs the little boy was placed upon. The female wolf had quite recently given birth to a litter of pups, and was feeling motherly. She saw the baby lying there alone and immediately thought, "Oh my, this poor pup has been abandoned." She quickly snatched the baby boy off the logs and took off into the forest. The mother saw the wolf just as she was disappearing into the forest with her son. She attempted to run after the wolf, screaming for her baby the entire time. But, by the time the mother climbed out of the murky water, the wolf was gone as fast as she had appeared.

The wolf raised the human child just as if he were of her natural born pups. As years passed, the once-fragile baby boy became more wolf than human. His fingers and toenails grew so long that they became twisted in bizarre designs, and his teeth were extremely sharp. He roamed the forest with the pack, and learned to survive just as a wolf does. He bent from the waist, because he was never taught to walk upright. He loved his wolf mother, yet had a nagging feeling that he belonged somewhere else with someone else.

One day while wondering the forest with his wolf siblings, he came across a raggedy shack. Near the shack, he saw a family of four. The wolf boy became completely mesmerized by the humans, and he had no idea why. He felt naturally drawn to them, and wanted very much to join the humans. He shook his head out of the daydream and returned to his nearby pack. His thoughts were crazy. He said to himself, "How could a wolf join a human family?" Yet every day he returned to his branch-covered spot to watch the little group, wishing he were one of them. After many months of this practice, he approached the mother wolf with his feelings. He said to her, "Mama, I really want to be with the humans that live in the forest." The mother wolf, by this time, had forgotten that the wolf she called son was really a human boy. She looked at her son lovingly and said, "Silly pup, you are a wolf, not a human. They would quickly run you off or worse. A wolf has no place in the human world, sweetheart." He knew the words his mother spoke were the truth. Wolves were often hunted because they threatened human pets and prey.

Yet he could not shake the feeling that he somehow belonged with them. The wolf boy spent the rest of his life looking at humans from a far, wishing deep down that he could be one of them, while thinking it impossible because he was a wolf.

Wallace D. Wattles wrote in his famous book, *The Science of Getting Rich*. "Thoughts are things." What you think in your head over time becomes your reality, which is good. Knowing this allows you to become aware that you have created in your life what's great, and what's less than great. In this moment you can decide to take control of exactly what shows up in your life. Our life stories begin with what we think. Thoughts create feelings that lead to "what we do" in our lives. What we do about what we think become the results that show up in our everyday lives. For this reason, whatever your brain thinks is always absolutely true for you. You believe yourself to be limited by circumstances, and you will live a life full of limitations. You will live a life quite similar to wolf boy – desperately wanting something else but thinking you are stuck where you are in the world.

The Lies We Tell

"Lying to ourselves is more deeply ingrained than lying to others." ~ Fyodor Dostoevsky

When you concentrate on what's not, you end up with what isn't.

A countless number of us are habitually compulsive liars. The worst part about this reality is that we are largely unaware. The unawareness is mostly due to how we classify the act of lying. We believe liars to be those that mean to deceive. These persons consciously fabricate events to lead others into believing untruths. We think liars do this because they want to achieve some personal gain or because they have developed the habit of lying. The problem with the common definition of lying is we think of it as something that must involve at least one other person. We rarely believe ourselves to be "natural" (because no one is born) liars. Therefore, many of us will spend a lifetime never telling the truth about our life choices and possibilities.

You can wander through life constantly tripping over every perceived unfair occurrence, swearing on a stack of bricks thirty feet high to anyone willing to listen that you are a victim. The people that do the best in life know there are no victims, just participants. First of all, much of what we dislike we created for ourselves. We choose the people with whom we hitch our wagons. You chose that husband or wife to start a family. You chose that job that you now profess to hate. You chose to eat the food that has made you several pounds overweight. Outside of death and other unexpected tragedies, we choose most of what shows up at the door. So why is it that we spend so much wasted time trying to convince ourselves that whatever's here is not our doing? I believe it is because we are constantly conditioned to find someone else to blame. We live in a climate of working to shield ourselves from blame. Just think of the number of times that you have heard someone say, possibly even you, "I'm not going to take the blame."

The avoidance of blame leads to the lies we tell ourselves, and gets between us and our goals. You can never win trying not to lose. That's what the act of blaming other people, circumstances, and for some even the way the wind blows, represents. You are working to avoid the responsibility of an outcome instead of working for the success of an outcome. This practice creates a perfect platform to start telling lies. Combine the desire to avoid blame with the Negative Nelly or Nell that resides in your head, and you are now infected with a contagious case of self-delusion with little hope of a complete recovery.

This is why it is so important to ask yourself in every situation that does not turn out the way you wanted, "How did I contribute to what happened, and what can I do next time to achieve a more favorable result?" Make a practice of telling yourself the truth in every aspect of your life. Tell yourself the truth about your relationships. Tell yourself the truth about your career choice. Tell yourself the truth about your life results. Then, do not waste one moment beating yourself upside the head about any of it. Get to work mixing up the cure, so you can enjoy the results.

If you were a screw up in the past, you're probably going to be a screw up in the future.

In my opinion, the foundation of self-development is that you can choose to be better today than you were yesterday. Self-development proves we are not chattel being unconsciously led by whatever "the random day demands." We can decide how we want to navigate our lives by improving our decision-making process. Instead of merely surviving whatever bumps up against us down the river of life, we can leave the mistakes we have made in the past back in the past where they belong. This new realization allows us to enjoy living fully. Now you are aware of you, and this awareness provides you the opportunity to live more of what your heart desires.

The breaking free of the past is absolutely essential to becoming the best you. I guess that's why every single self-development practitioner I have followed emphasizes "letting go of the past." Yet it's precisely this message that kept me stuck for a long time. The idea that you can simply decide to let go of things you did sounds absolutely amazing. The reality is a little more involved than just deciding to consciously let go. For this reason, the message can often lead to increased disappointment, and ultimately may lead to abandoning self-improvement altogether.

You can have a vision board nailed to your front door, or your declaration of decision taped to your bathroom mirror like me. You can say affirmations a thousand times a day, only to find yourself still stuck in a sticky mud of limitations. It's your past patterns that got you what you have in life. That's all of the good decisions and actions, and all of what you would like to forget. The patterns in your life can be like an invisible wall that you keep hitting. You slow down your run to pay more attention, and hit the wall. You write out an elaborate plan to get around it, and hit the wall anyway. You totally change the direction you're walking, and still hit the wall. Nothing you do stops you from hitting this darn invisible wall. You can't figure out what you're doing wrong. Goals, affirmations, mission statements, etc., are the methods we are told to use to get around this wall. Unfortunately, no one ever informed the wall so the wall still stands taking every blow you can throw.

In reality, the wall is visible. It was never hidden from any of us. You are simply incapable of finding what you aren't seeking. You are seeking to change "the what you got" and ignoring the "how you got." The plain message "that your past does not equal your future" is misleading. It is the separation of fruit and root. What you have gotten thus far is the fruit, and your patterns are the root. You must look in your past to find the patterns that yielded your present fruit. Patterns that, left untouched, will determine future fruit.

We can have the best of intentions to change something in our lives, only to end up falling prey to a self-defeating pattern. We do this by thinking that we are only required to decide on change and everything will fall into place, but then we later feel badly that we failed at goals we really wanted to accomplish. For many, it's the very advice that should have catapulted you to "being the best you," Which is the advice to live in the "Now" with no examination of the past. You may feel warm and fuzzy on the inside at first, but it will come to bite you in the butt.

I totally bought the hype, and was extremely drawn to the releasing-your-past concept. I had spent way too much time making changes to events that are impossible to change. Thinking that if I had made a different decision about this or that, I would now be enjoying a different outcome. Then, I would feel badly that I had made the wrong decision. Feeling badly lead to me mentally beating up on myself for perceived

YOU WILL HAVE TO BE NEW TO DO NEW

stupidity. These feelings were without advantage in every area of my life. I felt less confident when future decisions needed to be made. This practice made me largely indecisive when it came to deciding on one thing or another. For some reason, telling yourself you're stupid fails to build self-confidence. My lack of confidence in my abilities was stopping me from doing what I wanted to do with my time here on earth. So, I jumped at the notion that you can decide to drop yesterday for today and keep it moving.

I find this concept needs a little tweaking to be useful for a lot of folks, and it needed more than a little tweak to work for me. It is true you can drop yesterday for today, however, you must first be aware of what you did yesterday to make permanent changes.

The Power of the Past

Many of our daily activities are rooted in perpetual habit. What we think, what we eat, how we brush our teeth, even the way we drive to work in the morning is habit. A friend of mine and I were going out to eat dinner. I noticed that she was using a longer route than required to arrive at the restaurant. I mentioned to her that there was a much shorter way to get to our destination. She admitted that her husband had already shown her a quicker route. Her words to me were, "I listened to him, but I go the way I know." She was comfortable with what she knew, and could care less whether or not there was a more effective method.

In life, we do things over and over again whether we are comfortable or uncomfortable. There is comfort in routine. Similar to my friend, we go the way we know for most of our lives. We are mentally held hostage by numerous thinking structures that no longer serve our needs, if they ever did. These ways of thinking dictate the way we live our day-to-day lives, and care little about our new goals and objectives. These thinking structures' (or patterns') deepest desire is to sustain themselves by any means necessary.

Taking a glance at our individual past behaviors can uncover these unconscious thinking structures. You can see what has stopped you in the past. Make immediate changes in your present to achieve different outcomes in your future. Look at your past from an external position, as if you were watching an actor play a role in a movie. This is important, because the first time I attempted to look into my past to identify patterns that had held me back, I ended up placing myself back into that moment in time, and feeling the same negative emotions. It actually felt like the event was happening right then, and I felt awful. I thought to myself, this can't possibly help me to be better in my life.

You have to see past events as separate from you. Imagine you are watching a movie with you as the star. You are sitting back, watching the drama unfold. At the end of the story, you can objectively come to conclusions on what went wrong. Once you run a few different movies in your head, you will be able to identify central themes, such as a certain type of man, people that subtract rather than add, time-wasters, and the "star's" overall environment. It is best to start with low-level past events that you can think of without getting emotionally sucked back into that place in time. Another technique is to envision your personal events as happening to someone else. This method will come easy to people that are imaginative. You become the writer and director of your own made-for-you dramas. I know you're thinking this sounds a little crazy. But trust me, the ability to see the patterns that hurt you in the past is worth its weight in gold.

Once you can see the past without being emotionally tied to the events, you can acknowledge the past for what it is – just something that happened. You can break the patterns that have been holding you back, but that you never knew existed. The past allows you to clearly see how you got to the present, and what you will likely get in the future with the same course in play. Just don't allow yourself to get stuck looking backwards. This will rob you of your energy to be happy in your present, and the ability to thrive in your future.

The Proof is in the Pudding

The "power of the past" allow us to tell ourselves the truth about where we are, and where we are currently headed. Looking at our past patterns, we can predict what our results will be if we fail to change direction. There are two kinds of people in this big beautiful world of ours: those that rip off the band-aid in one quick pull, and those that prefer to slowly peel it away piece by piece. If you are reading this book, then you are a rip the band-aid off type of person. You want to know what's stopping you from getting what you demand of life or what's blocking your view of what you really want.

Once you tell yourself the truth about where you are, write it down in a journal. That way, you will be able to recognize the pattern when it shows up. Otherwise, you risk walking through life blindly making the same mistakes, and finding yourself constantly getting stuck in the same spots regardless of the best laid plans. For example, say you are the kind of person that has really great ideas. You love coming up with new business ideas or careers. You are really excited in the planning stages, but are unable to properly implement your ideas. Maybe you start on what you want to do, but never seem to finish what you start.

There's always a valid reason in your mind about why the best course of action was to abandon your creative idea. The problem is that every idea ultimately ends up in the wastebasket of "coulda," "woulda," "shoulda." Now that you have identified the pattern of this behavior, you can deal with it. You can make a "no matter what commitment" to complete the very next idea you decide to act on. Additionally, you can make the decision to only commit to what is truly meaningful to you. By choosing only what is meaningful, we are working to insure continuous inner motivation to accomplish what we say we will .

The Beginnings of Delusion

Here's proof that there is power in examining your past behavior. Look at those in your immediate circle. Pick one person for your "Is there power in the past experiment?" We all have at least one "Clearly Claire" hanging around somewhere. Clearly Claire (or Clearly Clint for the guys) is that one person for whom you can write out exactly where they're going to be a year from now. You could literally be a psychic when it comes to Clearly Claire. No matter what she says, you know exactly how things are going to turn out for her.

The truth is that you have no supernatural abilities in predicting the future. You are simply looking honestly at her patterns and habits. You know that if Clearly Claire is unhappy in a bad relationship with a certain someone, six months from now she will still be miserable if she is in the same relationship. Let's add to the mix a history of choosing the wrong men. Now you can comfortably prophesize even if she ditches Mr. Wonderful. She will probably replace him with a man that is equally wrong, and quite possibly worse. Looking at past and present patterns to determine future outcomes works in almost every area of life.

Let's look at Clearly Claire's employment situation that she complains about all the time. She hates being in what she considers to be a dead end job. Her bills are months behind, with no way of catching up in sight. Clearly Claire tells you on a regular basis how she is going to find another more fulfilling, higher-paying position. Yet she has been working at the same place for a number of years with no exit strategy. According to Claire, she also has no time, because of kids and work, to take any classes that would increase her job skills. Clearly Claire talks about what she would do "if she could" quit her job. She claims that her search keeps coming up empty. Or that she is only ever offered positions in the same line of work. She paints herself into an impossible corner, at the same time asserting things will change.

You know a year from now Clearly Claire will just have more unpaid bills to complain about. She will be in the same dead-end job, or another one exactly like the last. You know the two of you will have identical conversations as last year. Claire will talk about what she would do "if she could," and you (being her friend) will listen, quietly thinking in your own mind, "Nothing in your life is going to change for you, dear." You come to this conclusion by looking at her past history. You probably wonder in the back of your mind why she doesn't see it for herself.

Here's the rub. The Clearly Claire syndrome is alive and well in many of us walking the streets today. We are like Claire – blinded by our personal patterns and histories, secretly wondering why we continue to hit the same walls. Telling ourselves (like Claire) that we have valid reasons for failing to make changes that would improve our lives while citing lack of time, proper support, money, or education as reasons why we are where we are. We make quiet empty promises that when our lives change in one way or another, we will then do things differently. These promises are how we delude ourselves into believing that we are one "better circumstance" away from living our dream. Or worse, that we will never live our dreams because we are trapped by impossible circumstances.

Some go to their graves failing to realize that they were born with the power to create the circumstances they desire. That no man, or circumstance, has the power to stop you from getting what you demand out of your life. The problem is that you only demanded from life what you believed to be realistic. The question remains, who determines what is realistic? Your thoughts determined what was realistic for you, thoughts that were based on your beliefs. These individual beliefs were then proven by your habits and patterns. This process created the perfect foundation to keep you stuck right where you were standing. This foundation has you, like Clearly Claire, telling the same "I would if I could" tale to any sympathetic soul that will listen.

I am not telling you that life is not challenging, and it can be downright hard at times. Many of us know all too well that even when our lives are going well, circumstances can change in the blink of an eye. We also know that we have no choice in how we come into this world. No one asked us what parents we wanted, or what childhoods would be most preferable. The beginning of our lives, our circumstances, came in the bag we were handed. The bag has one instruction when you look inside: Work with what you got. There are no guarantees when we decide to marry the man or woman of our dreams that love will last a lifetime. The only promise that we are given is the opportunity of love that can last a life time. Often we will want to do something that no one can see, except us. But that's okay. As my mental mentor

Lisa Nichols would say, "God only gave the vision to you." We must be committed to our willingness to act, despite what we see, to claim what is personally meaningful.

What I am asserting is that all we need in life is opportunity, willingness, and ability. The best part about these three essential characteristics is that everyone possesses them. That's right. If you are currently breathing, you have the opportunity, willingness and ability to succeed in whatever you choose. You need only remove the invisible walls that stand between you and what you demand out of life. The circumstances in our lives are what they are, but you are not your present circumstances. Many of us unknowingly allow our circumstances to dictate to us, instead of dictating our circumstances. Then we tell ourselves convenient lies of why new action is impossible or isn't worth the effort. Our current habits and patterns are comfortable even when they do not serve our deepest aspirations.

This is why harnessing "the power in the past" is so important to permanent change. It shines a light on the choices you have made, and continue to make. You must use the lessons the past has to offer without dwelling or beating up on yourself. You avoid this natural instinct by accepting the truth that you made the best decision at the time with the level of awareness and knowledge you possessed at that moment. We do as well as we know to do, or are emotionally able to do.

By practicing this one activity with regularity, you actually live more of your life in the present. It stops you from bringing negative past habits into your present life. You also get to see what's working and serving you well, and that allows you to take what's working into every part of your life. Often, our best qualities become invisible to us when we ignore the past. Abilities such as how downright resourceful we can be, if and when we choose. The past is a tool available to us that we can use for our benefit. You just must be sure to use the tool properly, "according to the accompanying instructions." The instructions plainly state, "glances at the past are strictly for informational purposes." Otherwise, the past is like a chainsaw in an unskilled person's hand: dangerous.

Thoughts Spread Like Weeds in a Flower Patch

I can vividly remember the day that I came to see the home I now live in with my family. It was cloudy, and I wasn't very enthusiastic. The moment a house hit the market it was literally snatched up within twenty-four hours. Several times, I viewed a home just listed and by the time I called the agent to make an appointment, the home would already be under contract. To be honest, the homes that were coming on to the market were only okay to start with. So the small inventory to choose from wasn't WOWing, to say the least. To make matters worse, they were all totally overpriced by an overheated market. So by the third month of these experiences, I had grown completely overwhelmed by the process. Yet this day, I was in for an unexpectedly pleasant surprise in my home search.

When I drove up, right away I thought the outside of the home was welcoming. The neighborhood seemed to be quiet and well maintained. Overall, it appeared to be a nice environment to raise a family. Once inside, the house was pretty typical of the other homes I had seen. It was thirty years plus old, and showed every bit of its groovy era. But the home had been well maintained and I had experience in updating houses. When the short tour ended, the agent smiled and said, "I have a surprise for you." My husband and I looked at each other as she led us out the back door. The backyard was positively gorgeous. There were matured bushes and flowers growing everywhere. The best part was they were completely maintenance free except for watering. What caught my eye most were these flowers called Four O'clocks. They were piles upon piles of pink flowers that were more than a foot high growing along the entire back fence. These flowers were absolutely beautiful, and they simply come back every year after winter.

I'm unsure if these Four O'clocks sold the house, but they made a big impression on me. Now let's fast forward to a year later. We happened to have a really bad cold spell that must have killed the flowers. Only a few plants returned the following summer. Therefore, I had to find seeds, which proved a bit challenging (I think because you are supposed to buy certain seeds early in the spring, and it was already late May). I replanted the flowers, and they came back pretty quickly. All should have been well. I had the plants back that had influenced my decision to purchase the house.

Well, I have three children, two of which are boys, who enjoy playing any sport that involves a ball. Imagine baseballs, footballs, and soccer balls always ending up in these beautiful flowers. Next, imagine these boys not so carefully going in to retrieve their balls. The Four O'clocks were looking like dead o'clock, ripped and stepped on. So in my great wisdom, I decided to simply remove the flowers by removing the entire plants. Problem solved. Well… no, the plants would not be removed that easily. For the last four years, these flowers have come up. I pull them out when they come up. We had another cold spell, they came up, and I covered the ground with a tarp to stop the growth by blocking out the sun. You guessed it. They are still coming up year after year. I did a little research, via plant forums, and discovered that Four O'clocks are actually weeds that spread like crazy. There are others, like me, desperately trying to get rid of these flowers with no luck. My advice after this experience is to never plant something in your life, or garden, that you wouldn't want to look at forever because you just might have too.

This is why it is so important to guide and control your thoughts and words. You are literally planting seeds in your brain that spring up in countless forms. Our thoughts dictate the actions we take and the feelings we have. Thoughts and feelings attract what shows up in our day-to-day lives. For the longest time, I had no idea that this connection existed. My thinking was, "It doesn't matter how I feel or what I really think about XYZ." As long as I get what I need to get done. The way I feel has nothing to do with anything. The action I take is what's important, and that's where I need to focus my attention. But that's indeed the problem. Your thoughts and feelings largely govern the effectiveness of your actions. You have to feel what you do, because you do what you feel.

For example, often I thought my problem was never having enough. The solution was to generate more money, or cut back on a few expenses. My personal thoughts centered on how something will always come up to take money away, or money is hard to get but almost impossible to keep in large amounts. These thoughts kept me grasping at straws. This strategy kept me barely solving the problems in front of me and constantly anticipating more to come. I was stuck only thinking of survival, or as many middle class people say, "Wanting to be comfortable." These thoughts and feelings kept me staring at the ceiling in my house, instead of stretching for the stars in the sky. The worst part is, this thinking robs you of the excitement of living life. You think only of putting out fires, rather than thinking and enjoying all your possibilities to create life exactly as you would like to see it.

It Is What It Is. Now What?

The majority of us have some area in our lives in which we feel trapped. You may feel trapped in a job, marriage, or a lifestyle. The weight has been pulling you down for years, but you believe that you are powerless to change the situation. There may be real concrete circumstances involved to explain why you hold the beliefs that you do. For example, you hate your present job and would love to pursue your passion, but you have kids and a spouse that must have food to eat, and a warm place to sleep every night. The salary at the job you hate completely pays or helps to pay for these vital life necessities. Most people in this situation will take the position that they are stuck, case closed. Successful people know there is no such thing as a trap; there are only circumstances to be considered. The circumstances can be physical like a job, past events, lack of money and education, or a habit of negative thinking. The approach is always the same: establish goals and achieve them.

Never waste time pondering why circumstances are the way they are, because there is nothing to gain in the why. The challenges we face in life are just part of the earthly human experience. Human beings have had challenges since the beginning of time, and there is no change in sight. Some challenges were handed to us, while others are born out of the bad decisions we make. In either case, these are challenges that we can work through. The upside is that less than ideal circumstances force us to grow into a stronger people. This growth is unfortunately lost on many of us because we concentrate on the pain of the situation.

A business partnership between a family member and I went sour some years back. To say that I was very upset would be the equivalent of calling the mighty Mississippi a small stream. This person lied to my face constantly about how the business was doing. To make matters even worst, they took unauthorized money out of the bank account to make the business look better, as if it were doing just fine. The lying regarding the health of the business continued for approximately a year, until a bill was mistakenly sent to me for the business.

"Whatever is done in the dark will always show up in the light."

I thought silently, I'll just go ahead and just write a check for the bill. No big deal, I will leave record of the payment for my partner. A week or two later, I received a notice stating the check had come back for Non-Sufficient Funds. I immediately called the bank, thinking that an electronic mistake had to have occurred. Now, when a teller picked up the call after what seemed like forever, my first impulse was to immediately tell them their system had a glitch. A small voice stopped me. Instead, I asked for a balance on the account. What I heard next caused me to literally drop the phone on the floor. An account that had thousands of dollars in it now had $5.34 remaining. My chest stiffened and felt heavy. I thought my heart was going to fall out onto the floor.

Once I was able to properly comprehend exactly what had happened, that someone I loved and trusted had deceived me over and over again, that every time we discussed the business they had looked me in the eye and answered with a lie, I was devastated. A lying business partner alone would have been devastating enough. I know there are no guarantees in business. Taking the calculated risk is the cost of an entrepreneurial path.

Someone blatantly deceiving you, especially someone close to you, should not be a part of that path.

I became very upset and resentful toward this family member. It was an extremely negative time, because I was angry every day. After many days of being stuck in a funk, I realized that I was starting to fall into a state of depression. These negative emotions felt like a heavy weight on top of me. I did not want sadness and anger to become permanent residents in my spirit. Then and there, I prayed to God to help me through this situation. I asked God for guidance on what I should do next with my life. I was spiritually led to begin reading self-improvement books. Next, I asked what I ought to be doing with my existence here on earth.

I read once that we humans ask the wrong questions, and therefore end up with the wrong answers. We say stuff like "Why me?" or "If I had that, I would." We don't ask, "What am I supposed to learn? How is this situation preparing me or what new skill am I learning?" My question was answered with what seemed to be vague answers, at first. I became still and waited for a clear answer to come. First, I was led to activities that I had enjoyed as a child. Right here is the moment my life's purpose to serve others began to come into focus.

"You can stare at a closed door so long that you never notice a new one has opened."

You can spend years, or often a lifetime, playing the role of a victim. Thousands choose to blame others for their undesirable circumstances, thinking that if they could prove it's not their fault, life will exonerate them from taking responsibility for the outcomes. They never realize that even if exoneration were possible to attain, they would still be trapped in a subpar life. Taking responsibility provides freedom to create what you want.

It is impossible for blame and creation to share the same space. Blame looks at the past for answers to the present; creation uses this present moment to build your ideal circumstances. Each day I spent blaming the other person for my conditions, I felt a little bit weaker, a little more unsure, and a little more fearful.

When I definitively decided to take responsibility for my outcomes, the innate power available to every human being was initiated. Responsibility opened my eyes to a complete truth. This kind of truth is unclouded by the need to blame. I had knowingly closed my eyes to signs that were pointing to potential problems. I hoped, on a subconscious level, that these problems would be taken care of by someone or something other than me. Honestly, I had failed my partner by giving them authority they were not equipped to handle. I made judgments based on what I wanted my partner to do instead of what they were honestly capable of doing. Making decisions on "what I would like" instead of "what is" had been pulling me down in other areas of my life for a long time. The time I was wasting in blame would have never delivered this vital information. Blame will keep your mind trapped inside of your present challenges with no visible escape routes.

The moment we decide to adjust our focus to see clearly the opportunity within the challenge, our entire world changes for the better. Challenges expose the characteristics that have been holding us back in other areas of our lives for years. A fear of failure will stop you from attempting new, life-enriching endeavors. A fear of being wrong will breed a mentality of endless indecision that will immobilize you, preventing the afflicted from seeking out alternative paths to reach their goals when current roads are blocked.

Successful people plow ahead and dismiss whatever comes up as part of life's process. In truth, an answer to "Why (fill in the blank)?" would do nothing to change the situation. Only unwavering, consistent action has the power to change anything you dislike about your life. You must view yourself as the source from which all your outcomes flow, both good and bad. Seeing yourself as the source forces you to take responsibility for your life. Taking responsibility for who you are presently, and who you become in the future will shed light on all of your characteristics, both positive and negative. You will then be able to use what is empowering. We can only use what we can see, and whatever we can't see uses us.

Many of us get stuck in one (or more) of three negative mental habits. If these habits remain unbroken, they lead to various degrees of stagnation and regret.

1) Turning Back the Hands of Time

Looking into the past for answers as to why your present looks as it does is a common occurrence. We believe that if the past could be changed, our current situation would be different. This belief, similar to what most of us believe, turns into a habit. A habit that places us in an unchangeable past that leaves no options in the present. The habit, repeatedly practiced, grows into a pattern of living. Undisturbed this pattern keeps us stuck in present behaviors.

We think, "If only I had not married him or her, took that job, had not become a parent, and had different parents or done better in school. My life right now would be much better than it is today." Next, you begin to imagine all the ways you would be enjoying your "might have been" life. Looking back drills you further into the past, which ultimately leads to frustration.

Happiness built upon a different past is unattainable, because science has yet to develop a time machine. Therefore, you become more frustrated and some depressed with your current life. Focusing on the past blocks present joy and creative possibilities.

"There is one thing we can do, and the happiest people are those who can do it to the limit of their ability. We can be completely present. We can be all here. We can give all our attention to the opportunity before us." ~ Mark Van Doren

In truth, we all do the best we can with the resources available to us at the time. The choices we make are based largely based upon the thoughts we hold in our minds. Consequently, one has to think better to do better. Improved thinking requires you to let go of the emotional effects of past experiences to grow as a person. It is impossible to grow your thoughts and still hold on to the past. One does not allow the other to exist. You do not want to become someone that spends all your present moments in "if only." These people become stuck in a negative pattern that stunts their growth as long as they allow this mentality to fester within their being.

2) Caught in Your Own Trap

Rocky Balboa's Inspirational Speech to His Son...

"When things got hard, you started looking for something to blame. Like a Big Shadow. Let me tell you something you already know. The world ain't all sunshine and rainbows. It's a very mean and nasty place and I don't care how tough you are it will beat you to your knees and keep you there permanently if you let it..."

The worst part about throwing a pity party is you always find people to come. This is one social function that people come from far and wide to attend. They want you to finish talking about what's wrong in your life, so they can begin telling you why they have it worse than you. Talking about what went wrong only serves to make you feel weak and hopeless. Where your focus goes, your energy will mostly certainly follow. Finding ways to justify what's going wrong in your life also doesn't help you. Justification helps you to feel better in the short term. The downfall is that justification rarely leads to improving your personal situation. You instead decide to accept what you don't like, or worse, you become depressed by the perceived lack of options. Justifying why you do nothing to change less than preferable circumstances creates negative emotional feelings. No one has ever felt better by making themselves feel worse. Living your truth allows others to live theirs.

Living a life of "I'm trapped, there is nothing I can do" breeds a victim state of mind. In this space, we rationalize that nothing is our fault. You begin to feel sorry for yourself and stop taking productive, life-improving action. Let's be clear. I am not saying the bad situations that have taken place in your past are your fault. I am saying the past is the past, and the only power it has, is the power you give it. The quality of your present life is your responsibility. Most of us are simply addicted to our sad stories, because they provide a sense of comfort. The problem is this comfort turns us into victims being preyed upon by life. The quality of your life is your responsibility; therefore there are no victims, only willing participants.

A victim mentality is quite similar to becoming addicted to a street drug. Each time you take responsibility away from yourself, you receive a short pleasurable "It's not my fault" sensation. The sensation makes you more comfortable in your self-pity. After all, what's going on is not your fault, it's the fault of the other person, or the circumstances, or the universe. Here is the rub: each time you invoke the victim mentality you subtract from your personal power. After each pleasurable sensation, you feel worse than before you did the "drug." Therefore you take another hit and another hit to feel good again, and each time you sink deeper into this habit of shirking responsibility, which becomes a rut.

What you need to know is that ruts are really myths. We have thoughts and we have actions born out of those thoughts. When we fall into a habit of thoughts and actions that are the opposite of what we want to show up in our lives, this process receives the label of a "rut," because whatever is going on has little to nothing to do with us personally. It's an outside circumstance. You are just the victim.

Anytime we become victims, we give ourselves excuses not to act. The more we fail to act, the worst our situations become. This results in a need to, once again, utilize the victim mentality to provide a short pleasurable sensation or "high." Ultimately, we become like a junkie chasing the next quick fix to ease the pain. Our lives become one excuse after another for why we are unable to change our circumstances. You literally sit in a hole you have dug for yourself, grasping at the next convenient excuse. Thousands of people live out their entire lives feeling as if they are a victim of a trap set by life. Decide here and now to take responsibility for the quality of your one life. Do this even when events occur that are beyond your control. Decide, I may not control everything that happens, but I do control my responses to what happens.

3) The Blame Game

A popular news website posted an article on the great places to work in America. There were different companies spotlighted, with a picture of the employee being interviewed. The employees would give details as to why they loved their job. They would list reasons such as overall work environment, benefits, ability to be promoted, etc. At the bottom of the web page there was a section to comment on the post.

One of the companies listed was a great place to work is an extremely successful mail delivery service. The guy (we will call him "Al") loved his position as a delivery driver. He raved about his employer throughout the short article. Al had tried for years to be hired at the company, because of the numerous benefits employees receive. He had applied with this same employer several times, never getting a call for an interview. Finally, he got a call to come in and was offered his current position. At the time of the post, he had already been working with the company for five years.

The comments on the article were pretty mixed in their opinions. Some agreed with Al, others completely disagreed with Al, and the rest fell somewhere in the middle. There was one comment or commenter in particular that jumped off the page. We will call her "Kelli." She seemed a lot more disgruntled than other commenters that had worked for the company in the past. She ranted on and on about how terrible it is to end up working for this service. Kelli actually accused of Al of lying to show his job in a better light than it deserved. She wrote so many words that her comment had to be continued in a second post. The most interesting part? Kelli never even worked for this employer that she was mercilessly tearing apart.

Kelli's husband had worked for the company for twenty-five years, before deciding to retire. He had held the same position as Al. Kelli blamed the company for all their children's birthdays that her husband had missed. The long hours, due to forced overtime, that he worked that kept him away from home. She complained about vacations that they never shared as a couple. Throughout her rant, she blamed the company for just about every misfortune they had experienced as a family. She said that her husband shared her hate for the organization. He was unable to quit during those years because of his retirement benefits. Kelli spent twenty-five years blaming instead of living her best life on her terms. She was addicted to her sad story, and the cost was her happiness. Now her husband is retired with his benefits, and she is still blaming.

Blaming someone or something for your life is really easy to do. Taking full responsibility for our lives is challenging. I have wasted a lot of time blaming one thing or another for why I was not able to pursue my goals. I blamed poverty, or lack of previous knowledge in an area, for taking no action. In reality, the component I lacked was courage. You have to be brave enough to look yourself in the eye and take steps forward. You will need to move forward in both your thinking and action. One without the other is like pushing a heavy cart with no wheels. You are pushing with all your might, but you aren't going anywhere. Many people will never take this action because it's downright scary. Even when the "same" is bad, it's still comfortable, because the average person has grown familiar with it.

You are different, you know "new" is scary and will take steps forward anyway. You want what lies on the other side: a new result. Maybe the first result will not be what you are looking to accomplish. It doesn't matter, because you are committed to moving forward until you reach your desired outcome. Individual failures or successes are simply part of the process, and should be viewed as nothing more than learning opportunities.

Resist the innate tendency to blame "individual failures" as a solid reason to stop doing what you are doing. Or worst, to never attempt to accomplish your goal in the first place. The practice of blame is closely tied to its first cousin – fear. We blame our childhoods, friends, personal circumstances, and whatever else is handy at the time. Blame and fear are like the chicken and the egg. No one knows which one came first. The blame game can lead to fear of making a mistake, because the blamer does not want to become the blamed. Being fearful can easily lead you to blaming circumstances outside of yourself for everything that happens in your life.

Scared people tell themselves the option to do something "new" does not even exist. They say, "I don't have enough time," "I'm too old to do whatever," "If I had the money," "If I had more education," and "I would if…" They focus on images of ideal circumstances instead of current circumstances. Thus, they miss out on advantages by staring too hard at disadvantages. I'm going to let you in on a little secret that's not really a secret: right this minute there is someone in the world holding a worse hand than you. They are living a life of their dreams, though, because of only one reason. They have decided to do so, and backed up their commitment with persistent action.

Most of us, have had the "Man, if I had what so and so has I would do such and such." My friends and I would literally have conversations like this that would last for hours sometimes. The conversations would always begin quite innocently. Someone would have read about a (by society's standards) successful person committing a stupid act. Or maybe a successful individual that we were acquainted had done something crazy. One of us in the group would say "Did you hear that.......?" and one by one we would all join in. We all contributed our own two cents to the pointless conversation. I might say, "Seriously, if I was lucky to have those great circumstances I would...." At some point, we would all give a collective sigh of, "It must be nice." We enjoyed the short high of our imagined accomplishments, and would then return to our "Who's got it worst?" or "Isn't it awful?" conversations.

Scared people love to see the rich, or the otherwise privileged, mess up. They say things like, "If I had what they have, I would do differently." Ideal circumstances are not the defining factor in a human being's success. Many lottery winners ultimately go broke after winning millions of dollars. Yet there are individuals with unimaginable struggles who experience the greatest accomplishments. The defining factor is the decision that failure is not an option. Nothing and no one will hold you back from doing exactly what you desire to do, if you decide that your desire is strong enough.

Here are three essential keys to opening your personal door to living a successful life. Every person who has achieved success has possessed these elements in one way or another. Remember, living a successful life is about living a life within your purpose, deliberately choosing the road you wish to travel rather than accidentally falling onto a path of least resistance.

Right Here, Right Now

For years, I convinced myself that there was a magical spot where life was perfect. This spot had both a physical and mental address. I thought if I had a different family background or different personal experiences, my life would be different (and better). Like maybe being born in another state would have improved my opportunities. In short, I spent a lot of time sitting in one spot imagining ideal circumstances while making no real moves to go out and create what I imagined. I truly believed that you had to currently be in a good "place" to get to an even better "place." I had no idea that people who are successful at living life manufacture their own circumstances. They take full, conscious responsibility for the direction of their lives. Responsibility puts the power back into your hands. In a responsible state, you will be able to act on life, instead of feeling as if life is acting upon you.

Taking responsibility makes you completely aware of your limitless possibilities. When you are responsible, you know that everything you need to be successful is within you. There is no need to wait to move to a new city, find another job, or get another partner to pursue your goals. You can begin "doing you" right this minute. I am not advising you to not move or improve your present condition in whatever way you deem necessary. I am saying that you must begin exactly where you are standing. The power to improve your life is within you and only you.

Write down ten goals you would achieve if the circumstances in your life were your idea of perfect. You should not consider if these goals are practical for this exercise. Now, pick the three goals that seem to you the most doable. These goals can be in any area of your life you wish to improve. You may want to improve your living experience by becoming more physically fit, starting a business, spending more time with family, finding that special someone, going to school, or any other area you wish to transform. Pick the one of the three goals that fills you with the most excitement, if you were able to achieve it. This is important because you are going after experiences, not physical attainments. This was a shift for me, because I thought it was totally about acquiring the goal at hand. You want the feeling that achieving your goal brings to you. For example, those who choose to get an education or specific skills training beyond high school desire the feeling of confidence about their future opportunities. They finish school for the feeling of completing what you start. It isn't for the ceremony or the piece of paper that gets stuck in your hands.

~ CHAPTER 15 ~

Procrastination +Hesitation=Stagnation (P+H=S)

Next, decide what you are going to do right now toward achieving your chosen goal. Right now means an actual action. Successful people get straight to the action, and plan as they go along. When something is working, they press forward, and when some part of their plan needs to be adjusted? They make the necessary adjustments and push forward. Successful people refuse to sit around fretting over every little detail. A formula that has kept me moving regardless of the situation is P+H=S. The longer you procrastinate, the more uncertain about your decision you become. Uncertainty causes you to hesitate when making a move. Ultimately, you become stagnate because you have no idea what the correct action to take might be. You decide to take no action because now you are too fearful to move ahead.

Taking consistent action is always going to be the correct answer. You must stay in the game of life if you want to win. Sitting on the sidelines waiting for the perfect moment is not playing the game. You must jump in with both feet. For example, if the goal that makes you excited is to write a book, start today writing the outline for your book, and tomorrow begin writing one of the chapters. The outline of the book can still be a work in progress while you are writing. The most important step is to get active, and stay active. Avoid getting hung up on doing something in a particular order. Consistent action is better than the best laid plans that never happen.

An Eye for the Big Picture

People successful at living life have an eye for the big picture. Their goals are right in front of them where they can see them. This is important because you will never hit a target you are unable to see. You can keep your goals visible by posting affirmations, your declaration of decision or mission statement, vision boards, etc. I personally have a vision book that I can take everywhere. My vision book is a three ring binder where I have cut out pictures of what I want to appear. I also write accomplishments and new goals in this book. I include whatever is relevant to the achievement of my goals. On my laptop, I have a folder labeled Daily Ritual where my journal, declaration of decision, mini vision board, affirmations, and weekly plan of action are kept.

Definitively decide what you want to do and get going. Action is better than a thousand plans that remain plans. You can literally plan yourself out of taking concrete action by sitting there attempting to account for every possible scenario. The best thing to do is create a short, immediately actionable plan. Start acting on your goals and make adjustments, if needed, along the way. Weighing yourself down in details blocks your path. It is difficult to see past possible challenges when sitting still. There is no momentum pushing you forward. Therefore, each new challenge that comes up becomes a new weight holding you down. This leads you to question whether or not pursuing your goals is a valid use of your time.

There will be three "friendemies" that appear the moment you definitively decide to do anything in life that stretches your current self-image. Circumstances, roadblocks, and fears are going to begin popping into your head. A circumstance, for example, is the desire to lose weight, but finding it difficult to eat right when you cook for the household. You will have to make a separate meal in addition to the one for your family. A roadblock may be the need for more education in order to get promoted in your job. A fear can be walking away from a relationship that is no longer serving you when you are afraid of letting go of what has become familiar. Circumstances, roadblocks, and fears distract many from the big picture.

I think of the three as a triangle because all three are permanently connected. Those who find themselves in the middle of this triangle quite frequently become trapped by their thoughts. These self-defeating thoughts keep them stuck in their circumstances, roadblocks, and fears. Say you want to move to a new town that would provide more career opportunities. First, you imagine everything great about your potential new experience. The new opportunities that will open up, the new place you will live, or the new people you will meet. Suddenly your dream is interrupted by what I call "reality." You may have these thoughts: I have never been completely on my own with no one nearby. I have no money to move somewhere new. I will not know one single person in this new city. What if my plans fail to work out? Circumstance: you have yet to move somewhere with no one close by. Roadblock: you are currently without the resources to move. Fear: your plan may fail despite your efforts. These three alone stop us from signing up for the race, forget running it.

Here's a little truth to guide you through these inevitable moments. Our possibilities are endless, even though our physical lives have an expiration date. You have one life to live exactly the way you choose to live it. Maybe what you choose does not turn out as planned. Choices can be signposts pointing us in a certain direction. Your destination can be further down the road. Yet without the signposts, you would be headed in the wrong direction entirely. A choice that turns out less than what you initially imagined is a misguided fear. We should fear becoming less than our God-given potential, potential that lives within each and every single one of us. Getting to the end thinking about everything we could have done, realizing that we had exchanged a passion filled life for self-perceived safety, this is a real tragedy.

This troublesome triangle is actually a great tool when used correctly. The fact that they show up means you are pursuing a worthwhile goal. You simply aren't stretching yourself if the troublesome triangle is M.I.A. You are still operating within your defined comfort zone with no opportunity for growth. Every accomplishment that you are proud of was accompanied by fear. You simply made the decision to grow through it. For you, what you were getting from achieving your goal was more important than your fear.

We all have predetermined comfort zones created by our beliefs, habits, and patterns. Most people stop when they encounter the first sign of discomfort, because none of us like to be outside of our comfort zones. A comfort zone is a mental boundary you set up in your brain. You feel secure when you are inside of your comfort zone. Any step outside of this imaginary boundary and you feel deeply uneasy. Comfort zones are really our personal expectations of the world surrounding us. As long as what we expect to happen happens, everything is okay. The minute our personal expectations (or the expectations others have of us) clash with reality, there is a problem.

Comfort zones never consider the happiness or sadness of their owners. People remain in unhappy relationships, jobs, and even poverty to maintain their level of comfort. We all deeply desire the feeling of security. Comfort zones provide the illusion of a secure space in the constantly changing world. Individuals that choose to stay in this imaginary land lose out on the experience of becoming something more. The natural inclination of the human being is to push forward. Look at all the innovations we have had in the last twenty years. From Internet to cell phones, we humans forever want to climb a new mountain. You will never become your potential staying within your area of comfort.

Stretching out of your comfort zone does not have to include bungee jumping, unless that's what you would like to do. You need only pick an activity that you have in the past talked yourself out of doing. Or one that you have promised to do when time or money becomes available. Go ahead right now and carve out the time including a definite date. Sorry, money does not get you off the hook this time. Make a plan to set aside necessary resources for your activity. For example, if you want to take a trip to another country, call a travel agent and find out exactly how much your trip is going to cost. Go get a passport, and start making a list of places you would like to see when you arrive.

Begin putting money aside for your adventure. Every step you take toward your goal gets you that much closer to accomplishing them.

Successful people make a habit of living outside of their comfort. They keep their attention fixated on the prize that lies on the other side. Breaking out of comfort zones instantly increases self-esteem, because you believe in yourself more. This provides you with proof that you can do whatever you definitely decide to do. You feel resilient and confident about your future choices. Taking action to break out of our comfort zones removes the one million "How can I's?" that float through our minds when we are standing still. We experience greater happiness acting upon our desires. It's almost impossible to feel sad when doing something you want to do.

~ CHAPTER 16 ~
When the Going Gets Tough...
You Learn to Become Tougher

Seeing the big picture means accepting your reality, the type of reality that propels you through your life goals, a reality unaccompanied by a mental prison that keeps you stuck in your circumstances, roadblocks, and fears. This reality makes you aware of pebbles that will appear on the road of life, preparing you to make necessary adjustments to ultimately get exactly what you want. This reality tells you that the going will get tough. Tough going has always been a part of the human experience. Imagined and unimagined challenges will pop up out of nowhere.

One (often unimagined) issue is that the people closest to us may be unsupportive of our new choices. The new choice can be career, partner, religious beliefs, starting a business, or a million other options. You must keep in mind that few people enjoy change in any form. The majority of people want the "things" in their life to stay the same. Nothing personal, you just happen to be one of the "things" in their life. Therefore, you remaining the same person you have been would be extremely convenient for them. Your current state fits perfectly into their perception of reality. They believe you are becoming some new foreign individual, and this is frightening.

Someone close to them changing is mainly frightening because the change forces the other person to look at themselves. The world is largely composed of people making a whole bunch of excuses as to why real change is impossible. We talk about what is holding us back or completely stopping our movement forward. Then we go out and find others to agree with our self-limiting perceptions. Now, we have a complete loop of negative reinforcement. We think the negative thoughts and then find others who confirm their legitimacy. The world is perfect, until you come along with your new ideas and shake the core of their perfect negative perception. They think to themselves, if you can do something new, maybe I can too. This realization is empowering for some, and absolutely terrifying to others. The new idea goes against their current belief structure, which is uncomfortable. The way they choose to handle the discomfort is what determines what group they fall into. Movers accept the discomfort as part of the growing process. Settlers cringe at the hint of discomfort caused by change, and do whatever it takes to get back to comfort.

Therefore, it is totally possible to have some people offer you real encouraging support, and have the other side of the aisle offer discouraging commentary. Attempting to change another person's mind is an absolute waste of your valuable time. One, because changing someone else's mind is impossible. Secondly, your success or happiness does not require their approval. At the end of your life, someone agreeing with your choices will not be one of your final thoughts. This is why your life focus must be invested in activities that bring you the greatest joy, instead of what provides others with the greatest feeling of comfort.

I had mixed emotions the day my passion to coach and motivate others to their personal greatness was revealed to me. For years, I had been encouraging friends, family, and even strangers to follow their callings. All that time, I never took the advice I was giving to others, saying you should never make excuses in one breath, and making my own excuses in another. Giving suggestions on how they could more effectively accomplish their goals, yet being afraid to uncover and accomplish my personal goals.

Numerous people had suggested that I consider speaking to others as a profession. Still, the idea of coaching had never seriously crossed my mind. Who am I to help others uncover their life's desires? I am denying my deepest desires. What can I offer to others? I was perfectly willing to allow my fears to keep me stuck playing small until I came face to face with what my mental limitations were cheating me out of. I was forced to change my life strategy, or live with being less than what I was being called to. To be perfectly honest, it was shear fear that led me to accept my purpose. I do not want to reach the end of my life wondering what more could I have done.

I told my husband first exactly what my plans were. He looked at me with a puzzled look on his face, which is indescribable. To begin, he had no idea that a coach, outside of sports, existed. This required me to explain what coaching entailed. Once he understood, he stared at me with the same level of bewilderment as before. Of course, he wanted to know how and if people made money in this profession. How did I plan to get clients, to make money? How much time would it take to put the whole thing together? The questions seemed to go on forever and ever, literally. The questions were extra difficult, because I honestly did not have answers to most of them. Although I was terrified, I knew deep inside that this was right for me. Unfortunately, I also knew the reading, listening, going to seminars and studying of thousands of pages on self-improvement would "X out" other income-generating activities. This part of the conversation was the hardest, especially without answers to his other questions.

Luckily, it will be unnecessary for you to explain your plans to most of the people in your life. The less they know, the less they will have to pick at. Express your ideas to those who show genuine interest in your plans. These people will act as your support system through difficult times along the road. And difficult times will come. A supportive group or person does make the bumps in the road easier to bear. Sometimes, there is no one in your immediate circle willing to support you. You will need to seek out other avenues to find support. A lot of the people I associated with had no interest in my conversations of self-improvement and what I was discovering. I joined groups on networking sites devoted to these interests. I ended up with hundreds of virtual friends committed to living their best life. They have served as support and gave me the encouragement I needed to press forward.

Your dreams are fragile when they are brand new to you. In these times, you have to be selective with whom you share your dream. Otherwise, you run the risk of being influenced by the limiting beliefs of others. They may have only the best intentions when giving their advice. Your loved ones want you to avoid emotional disappointment, loss of money, or time. These are well-meaning, caring-filled thoughts. Intentions aside, their advice is useless and potentially dream killing unless they are giving effective suggestions on how to achieve your goals. We rarely, if ever, regret the things we attempted, it is more often the abandoned, un-attempted desire we regret.

The main point is to protect ourselves against any negative influences from those surrounding us, the well-intentioned people, and the not so well-intentioned people. What your peers, and even relatives think of you, isn't part of "the big picture." On the contrary, listening to their thoughts can block your view of the picture altogether. Ignore the opinions of others, because everybody has an opinion. Our results are born out of the actions we take. Another's opinion has no bearing on our ultimate success or redirection sign-posts. It would be great if the people surrounding you all decided to support your choices without judgment. The truth is, some will, some won't – that's the way life works. There are strategies we can utilize to get through these inevitable moments.

Honest + Action=Different

The moment you tell those around you what you plan to do differently in your life, they will say that you are changing. You are not the person they have known. They are right. You are someone that is finally being completely honest. You are now telling the truth about what you want out of life, regardless of your fears. No more shrinking from what's inside of you to get along with those outside of you. You are making a change to what was the status quo in your life for something new. You may have no idea exactly what the new will be. You simply realize that being honest, plus action, equals different, and you have decided to have different. You know that the only way to get where you want to go is to move. This is true, even when you have no idea what direction to take.

Sooner or later, forward movement is going to get you where your heart wants you to go. I use the term forward movement; because some people are constantly moving, yet they seem to inevitably end up in the same spot. These people play a game of musical chairs with their lives, except no chairs are removed from the circle when the music stops. They merely move from one chair to another hoping to discover something new in yet another chair but forever coming up short because all of the chairs are in the same circle. These are the people that hate going to their jobs day after day. Even if they get a new job, it is fundamentally the same job in a new place. These people are unhappy in their intimate relationships for a host of reasons, but they enter another relationship with someone new that is similar to their last mate. These people complain about their upbringing and later make the same mistakes they accuse their parents of making. These people are shocked when they get the same results from the same actions. These people are totally blinded by their life patterns.

You may attempt to please the world, but what does it matter if you didn't please the only one that ever really mattered? You.

In the beginning, your decision to be "honest" about what you want is fragile. Only discuss your dreams with those willing to listen. First, you must qualify your "dream supporters" before you start spilling your guts. The people that respectfully listen to your plans with "no extras" are "dream supporters." Some of these "dream supporters" will be so excited by your plans that they will offer to help you. Some will give you words of encouragement that help to keep your spirits high. Others will be so inspired by your truth that they will begin pursuing their dreams. The positive energy from your dream supporters will serve as further encouragement to you.

Some of my friends and family were highly supportive when I felt comfortable enough to share my dream of inspiring others to live their greatest life. Others were, let's say, intensely concerned about this decision to stop settling for what I had convinced myself I could get or what makes the most sense to do, to realize that you can get almost whatever you set your mind to. I remember crying the first time I said it to someone. Saying it out loud made me feel as if this great weight had been lifted off my shoulders. I was standing in the light of my divine truth, instead of the shadow cast by the opinions of others. This truth had been patiently sitting inside of me waiting for my acknowledgement. Now, it was out in the sun.

The encouraging group was great with their positively-charged comments: "I'm sure you will be successful" and "Well, life is all about setting out on new adventures here and there." I felt happy that I decided to share. Now for the other side, which included some of those closest to me, people that I would have never expected to be critical, downright hurtful, to use words such as stupid and pointless. These people would constantly ask me the same questions over and over again, "What exactly are you doing again?" or "Why do you want to do that?" or "Do you honestly believe that will work?" At first, I would repeat my reasoning hoping they would become supportive. Or at the very least, get tired and stop asking the same questions. I soon realized they were going to continue to ask these questions and have negative comments. They were waiting for me to say, "I changed my mind, what was I thinking?" A changed mind was the only answer they were interested in hearing.

Be careful, some people will listen to your plans or ask questions only to criticize. They want information merely to tell you why your plan will fail, and offering no helpful suggestions on what could be adjusted to make your idea more feasible. These people will help to intensify your fears and increase the negative chatter in your head. Some speak from a place of their own fear of venturing out to pursue a passion. Others wholeheartedly want to help you avoid being disappointed if your plan later needs to be reworked. They believe the desire not to lose is the same as the desire to win. They are incorrect in this thinking. Working to not lose will most certainly reduce the real life actions that you take. You end up over-analyzing every potential action. Ultimately, you talk yourself out of making goal-achieving moves and end up immobilized, running a trillion "What if the worst happens?" scenarios in your head. Scenarios like these are generated by your personal fears and the negative chatter provided by your non-supporters. Here's what you do when failure occurs: Keep Going. You must be able to accept failure as part of the process to achieving your intended goal. The only real fear you should entertain is getting to the end of your life feeling unfulfilled.

The Right Tools Are Worth Their Weight in Gold

Find objective people to talk over your plans with and receive inspiration. Read inspirational material daily to keep your motivation levels high. John H. Johnson, the creator of *Ebony and Jet Magazine*, and the first African American to make the *Forbes* 400 list, attended school during the day, and concentrated on self-improvement at night. In order to achieve success, you must keep your goals in front of you. That means hitting your goals from all sides, because you are going to need to. Life has a way of blurring our vision, even when our goals are worthwhile. In the beginning, you are really excited about your goals. Then the big chill hits, and your once-on-fire excitement begins to cool. The chill is caused by doubts, present obligations, and keeping up the status quo. This is fine because we know that all worthwhile goals are going to be a great deal of work.

This is the type of work that allows you to feel an immediate internal return, but you won't see an immediate external return. Without the proper support, you may quickly slip back into old habits, especially when those with whom you spend the most time don't share your vision. Reading and listening to inspiring material and talking to people that are interested in your success is essential. Most women have underwear drawers in their bedrooms – I have book drawers. I ran out of room on my book shelves, and they had to go somewhere. Changing your thinking takes everyday conscious learning on your part. You have been mostly unconsciously learning your entire life. This is true whether you are eighty years young or eighteen.

The fears and self-limiting beliefs of those closest to you have been planted in your brain and have taken root. Now you must pull each plant out by their roots to insure they are totally removed. Repeating positive affirmations without changing what influences enter your brain may help you to feel better in the short term. But they will not change your visible outcomes in the long term. It is like pulling the leaves off a weed. The weed may look better, even appear to be gone, but in a short time it will be back as strong as ever. The root of the weed is still in the ground, and therefore the plant lives. You can say whatever you want out of your mouth, but you have to plant a new seed in your head.

Plant a self-expanding belief in the new fertile farmland of your brain after removing the weeds. A focus on self-development pulls out the roots of your negative thinking. You can find self-development mentors in inspirational books, audio recordings, and videos. I love reading biographies on people that have accomplished greatness in their lives. It feels as if they are sitting with me sharing their truth.

You can use their stories as roadmaps to accomplishing your goals, regardless of what they are. You can use these lessons to become a better everything, from business mogul, to better friend, to an overall more peaceful soul. You will begin to find yourself asking for your mentor's advice in your head. Sometimes, I ask myself what Lisa (Lisa Nichols) would do. What advice would she give to me right now in this situation? The best part, you will actually hear answers that come as thoughts in your head when you ask.

I was terrified at the thought of being totally exposed to the world. Being your authentic self can be an uncomfortable endeavor, to say the least. I must have listened to the book *Success Principles* by Jack Canfield hundreds of times. So, I asked Mr. Canfield what to do. In my mind, he told me to scale down the risk. Maybe, I wasn't ready to expose myself to thousands that minute. But I could begin sharing my stories and thoughts with a dozen, and build from there. These activities, consistently practiced, will fuel your energy to persist in all weather conditions along the road to success.

Right now, begin creating your go-to group. These are real people and people that you admire through their teachings. Your physical group, you can call when you're feeling as if you might quit. Your imagined group is even more available, because you can call on them twenty-four hours, seven days a week. This person or persons can be anyone you feel encouraged by. It's nice when close family and friends can be in this group. Sometimes, however, those closest to you will not share your vision. No worries. Connect with those that do.

These can be people with whom you worship, a mentor, those in your community, or others on a similar path. You can find supporters on networking sites tailored to your specific interests. There are billions of people on this planet, and modern technology has placed them right next door. What is most important is to find people that spiritually lift you up, rather than pulling you down.

It's important to note, this advice is about what you should do to get the best results in your life. You are responsible for you. This should not be taken as a platform to blame other people for your un-taken actions. I personally learned this lesson, and still must frequently remind myself, "My life, my responsibility." Blaming others for your stalled personal achievements is a habit much too easy to fall into. I often found myself blaming my husband, family obligations, and plain day-to day-living. It felt really good in those moments to excuse myself from responsibility, to dream of everything I could accomplish if those around me were simply "better." Sadly, the "good moments" were often too quickly replaced with feelings of disappointment. Over time, this disappointment grew into a lack of confidence in my actual abilities. Truth is, the more you do in this world, the more you believe you can do. The less you do in this world, the less you believe you can do. Two keys to success are real action and the decision to take complete responsibility for what you accomplish.

~ CHAPTER 17 ~
Fall First

Fear can be a nasty little emotion that has more than once left me paralyzed. You may know exactly what you want to do in your brain. You may plan out exactly what you need to accomplish your goal. You may say a million affirmations and have them pasted all over your walls, or in my case bathroom mirrors. Yet for some reason your great idea stays exactly that – a really great idea. You say to yourself, "The abilities to accomplish this goal are within me." You wonder why you are unable to get started on your plans or, when you do get started, why you ultimately just stop.

The root cause of why many of us aren't able to see our dreams materialize is because of fear. We fear failure, looking stupid, loss of money, loss of approval, and the list continues. In my situation, I was afraid of losing my potential story and respect. All my life, those in my life had spoken of what great potential I possessed. What if I am nothing more than "great potential?" What would those closest to me think about what I want to do? What if I fail so miserably that I won't have my potential story?

The problem with fear is that you really can't fight it, because fear is a phantom. Fear is a ghostly figure that roams the awaiting hallways of your mind. The phantom halts the best laid plans with imagined pictures of certain doom. We have all been conditioned (probably by those who loved us most) to follow the status quo. They did this in an attempt to protect us from failure and heartbreak, thinking if they convinced us to follow their version of the straight and narrow, our lives would turn out great. Any step or even any thought outside of "what's expected" summons the fear phantom.

How to Get Pretty: The Art of Attracting

In simple terms, The Law of Attraction states that like will be attracted to like. Learning to attract exactly what you want instead of what you don't is an art. You attract what you think about all day. Much of what you think is probably rooted in frustration and fear. If you are going to reap abundance and peace in your life, you must sow new thoughts of abundance and joy. We are all familiar with the cliché, "You are what you eat." The Law of Attraction says, "You are what you think."

Your life is the sum of your dominant thoughts. The first time I ever heard The Law of Attraction was some years back when I read *The Secret*. I read a lot of stuff on the Internet talking about *The Secret* so I bought the book to find out exactly what is *The Secret*. Monique's interpretation is that through belief you can create whatever you want through active focus, energy, and expectation. Still, I didn't quite get how you bring what you want most out of your imagination into life. I mean, if you imagine a million dollars it usually doesn't magically appear in a briefcase in the middle of the living room.

That said, I believed in the The Law of Attraction almost immediately without fully understanding it because of something that occurred as a child. I remember this one experience at nine years old that convinced me that somehow we humans could make what we want happen. Each year my elementary school had a kiddie debutant ball. One girl from each class would be given the honor of wearing a white formal gown. A boy from each class would be chosen as her escort across the stage. The individual teachers decided how their students would be chosen. Some teachers had their students vote, others chose their favorite students, but many simply put each student's name in the hat and pulled. My teacher preferred the last method, and so each of us nine-year-old girls and a few boys (though the boys weren't as excited to dress up as the girls, big surprise) wrote our names on a piece of paper that would be thrown into a hat.

I deeply desired to be chosen to participate. Going to an inner-city school, there weren't very many exciting activities. I had been chosen four years earlier and it was the highlight of that year. The names were drawn, and no, my name wasn't magically called. The girl whose name was called, however, decided she no longer wished to participate. Sitting at my desk, I closed my eyes and focused on hearing my name called with every fiber of me. It felt as if no one else was in the room, just my desire and me. Over and over in my head I heard and saw my teacher's lips form the name Monique, Monique until the teacher actually said, "Monique!" I was so engaged in this image that I had no idea that she had actually called my name. I thought the voice was still in my head. A girl hit me in the shoulder, and said "Monique, she called your name." I looked up at my teacher in disbelief and asked, "Did you really?" Then and there I knew that somehow I had influenced what happened. Of course, as I got older, with my adult mind I dismissed the experience as random luck. Yet deep down I believed that somehow I had brought a dream into reality. I had attracted exactly what I deeply desired into my life.

Honestly if you look around there are lots of everyday examples of like attracting like. Happy people hang with other happy people, grumpy people hang with other grumpy people. Rich people hang out with other rich people. Those with a faith in a higher power hang out with others in faith. Even from a practical perspective, businesses are created on the platform of attraction. Business owners believe their products or services will attract patrons that want what they are selling. Over and over again, what's like seems to be drawn to itself. I'm sure you can think of at least a few examples yourself. Many of your friends have similar interests to yours – that's what attracted you to those friends. Even our incomes are attracted. Research has shown that most of the people we know earn the same or close to the same money we do.

On the other side of the equation, there are numerous critics of The Law of Attraction. Some say that it is the equivalent of "Hocus Pocus," magic fairies granting wishes to those true few believers. Believing that what you think about will show up out of thin air. Remember, my million dollars appearing in the living room example. I now, after further study, believe this to be a misunderstanding of the Law. We live in a physical universe so nothing occurs without action. Even at nine, there was action that got me into that ball. I put my name in the hat. I came to school the day the names would be chosen. I was prepared for the opportunity when it came. Sitting in your room seeing that million dollars in your head isn't going to get you anything but frustrated. Come on, even lottery winners must go out and buy a ticket. You have to create what you want in your life with movement toward what you want. This active focus is what you need to have if you are going to attract your dreams.

You can create the biggest vision board or write the clearest declaration and absolutely nothing will happen without action. I didn't make these rules. They were here when I arrived. This is why some believe the Law doesn't work. They create these huge vision boards with pictures of Oprah, mansions, expensive cars – while working at Subway. I love Subway, but if that's your only plan to become a multimillionaire, you probably aren't going to become a multimillionaire in the next decade being a sandwich artist. You could become a multimillionaire over a longer period of time with any job. You would need to focus your energy in that direction, and take action to save and invest on a committed schedule. Let's tell the truth. If you really want to increase your income you must do something more than you are presently doing. What's great in your life and what's less than great is a result of what you focused on and acted upon. To have anything different in your life, you must do differently.

Others derail themselves when going after what they want by beginning with what they don't want or can't do. I had a client passionately explain to me why she had to lose weight because she was morbidly obese. In the same conversation, she told me that she had no time to exercise and had to cook for her family. She said her family wasn't going to eat food with reduced calories because of her choices. So it was impossible for her to change present eating patterns because, "I have no time to exercise, I don't have time to prepare a different meal just for me. But I do really need to lose all this excess weight. I have even bought a size eight dress to hang in my closet because that is the size I am attracting."

Now, this mental position is the desire to having magic fairy dust sprinkled on top of your head. You cannot get endless possibility while actively affirming impossibility. Like energy will always attract like energy. Wanting to release weight while believing it is impossible to release weight is unlike energy. Your deep-down belief is the energy you are sending out into the universe. If, like my client, you are sending out "I can't lose weight" energy into the universe, then guess what happens? You fail to lose weight and say the Law of Attraction doesn't work. Or, if you affirm out loud that you will accomplish your goal while secretly believing it is impossible, the Law of Attraction will draw to you exactly what you believe. It is crazy to think you can place your focus in 'don't want' and 'can't get,' but still want and can have.

This state of conflicting energy is very common when we have a desire that reaches outside of what we currently possess. The minute we imagine stretching beyond what we can see, A thousand reasons why what we desire is going to be extremely hard or impossible to acquire will show up. This is actually a great sign to you, because it means that you have made a choice that pushes you outside of your self-created comfort zone. We spend our entire lives building a prison around ourselves. This prison is made out of our conditioned comfort zones and keeps us stuck right where we are. Each time you want to do something outside the bars, you will have to stretch your cage. Just like real bars that are made of steel, this task can seem impossible. If you keep your eyes focused on what's outside the bars, you will do what it takes to reach your goals. On the opposite side, if you choose to keep your eyes focused on the bars, which are the challenges that inevitably appear, you will never break free from your cage because it's what's outside the cage that provides the motivation. If you focus and reach for what's beyond the bars, those same bars that have been holding you back will disappear.

It's great to know that you have a goal that stretches you, but how do you achieve it? How do you stop the voices in your head from stopping you? First, we have to become aware of what these voices are and what these voices are not. These voices are our manifested fears speaking out loud to us. These voices are years of hearing more 'can'ts' than 'cans.' These voices are usually not signs that we should abandon the desire. If what you are afraid to do is a dream of yours, take another step right now. I truly believe that dreams are divinely provided for a reason. Sometimes, the reason is to teach a lesson you otherwise would not have learned without the dream, a lesson that may lead you to your authentic dream because often our dreams are created out of what we think we can have. Therefore, your dream can become riddled with conditioned limitations. A dream tamed with limitations is inauthentic, because dreams come from your inner spirit, which is limitless. It is impossible to create the limitless in a limited space.

Your inner voice may alert you to pause and outright stop when you should take another direction. But this usually occurs when what we want is created out of factors outside of our control, or when we are confused about the real dream, such as wanting to love a certain person or wanting a particular job. That man you desperately love may be completely wrong for you.

What you control, and the real desire, is to be in a healthy love affair with someone that feels exactly the same way. Now let's call him "Bob." Bob says he wants a healthy love relationship with you. Then he just may be Mr. Right. If you feel less than exceptional, however, being in a relationship with Bob, then that's probably your inner voice nudging you with an elbow to get far away from Bob.

Or let's say you want this management position in a company where there is little room to advance. But you limit yourself by saying the only way your desire can be satisfied is for you to get promoted in this company at this certain location. Your desire may never happen, because your divine promotion maybe in another company or another city. Ask for what you want to show up in your life only and let it go. Ask for a promotion, ask for love to come into your life, ask for clarity about your next step and stop. Release the urge to place conditions on how your desires are to be met. There may be a better way for you to have what you want than you think.

There is a quiet place that resides in every one of us that is untouched by years of negative conditioning. For me, this place is the piece of God that resides in me. Our true spirit is pure and untouched. If you practice quieting your mind through scheduled meditation, or sitting quietly each day, you can connect to this limitless always-truthful part of yourself. The more you connect with your spirit, the more you are able to tell the difference between what fear is and what is good inside advice. You will be able to make definite decisions quickly, because you will feel when it's right and when it's wrong.

Successful application of the Law of Attraction requires intention and alignment. You first have to set your intention to have or do whatever the goal is. Intention is defined as, "An aim that guides action; an objective." Set the intention first and align your actions with your declared intention. Sift all your focused actions through an "Am I going toward or away from the objective?" filter.

Alignment is the physical work that must be done. These are your focused actions.

You Can Forget What You Think You Know

Setting your intention, and aligning your actions, sounds too simple to work. It can't be simple because then the whole world would be attracting their wildest dreams. Remember, you have to connect to the limitless place inside of you, a space that has been being filled with limitations, insecurities, and various forms of "I can't have" your entire life. To cement these beliefs, you have gathered examples from your surroundings to prove that you are indeed correct. You think you can't have the position in the company you desire. You say, "Troy has been working here for ten years in the same job. I'm telling you nobody moves up in this horrible place." Even if the same day you speak these words somebody gets promoted after only working for the company two years, you will grumble, "They know someone at the top."

Long story short, when you set out to attract what you want (while secretly believing it is impossible), you will either fail to create what you desire, or worst you will create its polar opposite through unintentional sabotage and negative emotions. One example of unintentional sabotage is when we lean into destructive habits such as procrastination. You want to start a business but put forth no real activity. Then you make excuses about how your life circumstance renders obtaining what you want impossible. Or spend most of your time working on minor activities that pay you with minor results. The true you will always appear. This makes it absolutely imperative that you get on purpose with what you want to attract. You have believed what you believe for a long time. Therefore, getting some new beliefs is not going to be an easy task. Especially when a lot of your beliefs are buried in your subconscious mind. So how are you going to achieve this lofty goal of yours? You are going to practice the beliefs you wish to have.

Adjust Your View

An investment in motivational seminars is great because you can hear speakers from different walks of life, from PhD's to recovering addicts. Hearing these stories in person makes them real to you. One speaker that left an impression on me was from a foreign country. He said when he arrived here in the US, he had no money, knew little English, and had no ideas. While watching television in the shelter with his wife, however, he became absolutely certain that he was going to thrive in this new land.

A talk show was playing, and when he heard the complaints of the guests he was shocked. They were complaining about their boyfriend and girlfriend relationships, while having hot water in this country was, for him, the equivalent of living the life of luxury. He said that right then, he looked at his wife in the eyes and said, "We are going to be alright because these people think they have problems." He suddenly began to think about all the abilities he actually had. He is now a successful business owner. Change your view from everything you don't have to everything you do. Opportunities and resources will seem as if they are magically appearing.

Do it Now, Do it Here

Our society has become absorbed with getting ready to do. Start today on whatever you are planning today. You can do this in any area of your life that you choose. If you to be a nurse, you can go sign up to be a volunteer at the hospital now. You can fill out the nursing school application now. The problem with a plan lacking immediate action is you may confuse planning for action. The thing you want to do can be done right where you are. You don't need to wait to move to a bigger city. Start where you are to get where you need to be. If you want to be an actor, there are plays to audition for and acting classes all over the country. You don't need to wait for funds to move to Los Angeles or New York. There are hundreds of YouTube stars making more than six figures a year, and some that have crossed the million a year mark with a digital camera and a dream.

You Will Fly as High as You Are

Your attitude determines your altitude in life, because your attitude has energy. That energy has a vibration, and you will draw only what has the same vibration. You are attracting what you are putting out in the world. Most of the time you are unaware of the vibration you are sending. You are reacting to whatever happens to you in the moment. You have an argument with your partner, and you will give an angry vibe all day. This is why simply thinking positive thoughts alone is insufficient. You have to create a joyful attitude if you are going to vibrate positivity. An attitude is more than a feeling, it is a state of being. A joyful attitude sends out an "I'm happy, give me more" vibe. This state allows the disruptions of life to roll off your back. A negative attitude absorbs every bad thing that happens, seeing each incident as confirmation that life stinks. Keep your energy as high as you want to be, and you will get to that place sooner than you think.

Speak It to Be It

Words are powerful creation tools. Using your words properly will allow you to enjoy your dream before you have it. First, decide that your words are going to now represent what and who you want to be. Reframe yourself from complaining about those elements in your life that are less than perfect. It is important to note that energy goes where attention flows. Refuse to complain for one twenty-four hour period. Any time the desire enters your mind, think of something you are happy about. Or you can create a mental picture of when you are most happy. I think of my daughter and I lying in bed together cuddling, and that picture brings me back to a happy place. Now let's create affirmations that reflect your desires.

Always work to state your affirmations in "I am" or "I will" format. For example, I will buy a new home right now by saving money every month. Now if you find it difficult to believe for whatever reason (maybe you are just wanting to hold your head above water) then change it to second person. "You will buy a new house by saving money each month. I don't care if it is a dollar you have to borrow to start saving, do it." The activity of moving on your affirmation, no matter the amount, stimulates both belief and excitement, which propels you forward. Say your affirmations twice daily, being mindful to keep your great attitude consistent. Last, keep your affirmations short and simple. Less words are easier to say and, most importantly, believe.

Greatness is Sticky

Get yourself a mentor for whatever it is you want to attract, through books or in person. This works in any area of your life. If you want to be a married woman, hang around happily married women. Go to lunch with them because dinnertime is usually already taken by their family. Greatness is a creative, ever-expanding fruitful tree that wants all of mankind to have a bite. That's why your married girlfriends are trying to hook you up. That's why authentically successful people love to tell others how to become successful too. Read books, listen to audio CDs, immerse yourself in what you want to attract.

Give up Hope Altogether

One of Oprah Winfrey's guests defined forgiveness as, "Giving up the hope that the past could be any different." The phrase "When the student is ready, the teacher will appear" is real. This was the first time I had ever heard forgiveness defined this way. This statement shook me right out of my socks, because the reason I had been unable to forgive had never been uncovered, at least to my eyes. I deeply wanted to forgive the grandfather that had cut me out of his life at twelve years old, the adults in my life that had let down the little girl I was once. I wanted to forgive myself for poor decisions that had complicated my young life. I took personal responsibility and felt better, but still couldn't let the stories go. I told myself that whatever happened had to happen for me to be the woman I am today. I felt empowered, but still couldn't talk about the past without being completely transported back to that specific moment in time, all those same emotions flooding back into me as if it were happening in the present.

Yes, I had read the outstanding inspirational material out there regarding techniques to forgive. Brian Tracy gives excellent advice in his book *Maximum Achievement* on letting go of what you are not over by writing "the letter." When I wrote the letter, however, the first time, it did little to ease my resentment. For some, making the decision to forgive and then writing "the letter" (which is fully explained in his book) is all that is needed to release them from continuing this life-wasting activity. Holding on to anger and resentment about something that already happened only torments you. The people that you are angry with aren't thinking about you at all. The worst part, if you brought whatever is eating at you up, their reactions would usually fall into one of three categories: 1) they have no idea what you are talking about, 2) tell you to get over it, or 3) begin denying any responsibility.

The greatest tragedy is that it is impossible to go forward walking backwards. Think about if you want to go to school, and you are past the traditional age. You may start thinking, "Well, if I would have gone when I was younger, I would already have X years in my career." So now you are focusing on wouldas, shouldas, and couldas, which have nothing to do with what you want to do. You start thinking about the decisions you made when you were younger, or you begin to resent your parents for not providing the money, or raising you to believe that additional education is not a priority. Whichever the thought (or a combination), you are sabotaging yourself with this bird's nest of negativity.

"Forgiveness is not always easy. At times, it feels more painful than the wound we suffered, to forgive the one that inflicted it. And yet, there is no peace without forgiveness." ~ Marianne Williamson

Or maybe, like I did, you are still harboring negative emotions about an event that took place in your life. You are allowing something that happened yesterday to affect your today. Give up the hope that the past could be any different, because, as a friend, I'm telling you it can't be. You are not letting the person that harmed you get away with murder. You are stopping the murder of a life peacefully lived. You can be angry every second of every minute of every day of every year until you depart your one life. Your anger will never turn back the hands of time. The clock keeps ticking, regardless of how you spend your time. Once you give up hope, you can in earnest decide to let the pain go. I believe then you can give the event or circumstance the funeral it deserves by writing "the letter." Here is the structure that I recommend:

Dear [NAME],

Start with the event that has caused you pain. Pour out all your emotions here about what you feel it has done to your life. The only catch is to make what you are hurt by short. I sincerely recommend one paragraph. Keeping it short accomplishes two extremely important goals to letting go. Limiting your words makes each one count, which forces you to get to the root of the pain. Think about it, if you have ever been given pain medicine intravenously, what works quickest? The pill you pop in your mouth that has to go to your stomach to get absorbed, to go to your blood stream? Or the pain medicine that you get through an IV, that's connected to your blood stream? Now that you are at the root, you can release the pain by telling them that you forgive them for what happened. You can also say that you are right now choosing to say hello to the gifts of the present by closing this last door to the past. In conclusion, wish them peace and happiness in their lives.

Love and Light,

[YOUR NAME]

Now destroy this letter you wrote, by ending the funeral with a burial. Tear the letter into tiny pieces that render the paper unreadable. Dig up a small patch of earth and drop the pieces into the ground. You can also throw it in the garbage outside in the trash that will be being picked up by the garbage man. Don't throw away the letter in your house if you choose this method. The purpose of the letter is to get rid of these emotions. Your emotions are energy, which you poured into the letter. So it is unproductive to have what you want to be rid of sitting a few feet away.

Until We Meet Again

"Our background and circumstances may have influenced who we are, but we are responsible for who we become." ~ Barbara Geraci

The best element of this one life that we live is that if we drift off course, we can consciously decide to get back on course. Or personally draw a whole new map that serves the person we want to be while keeping what's already great about who we are. There is nothing broken inside of us that needs to be fixed. We are powerfully, divinely created beings that already possess the resources we need to accomplish any goal. Often we need help uncovering these qualities due to limiting beliefs that we have internalized as fact. One book, one CD, or one coaching course is not enough to break down mental walls that have been built since the day you were born.

You will have to dedicate yourself to continuous self-growth if you are going to consistently live a life drawn by your dreams, instead of one colored by your fears. And I know you will, because you picked up this book, which proves you want more. And the desire for more life is the first step to getting on purpose. We can choose to live in the light of awareness instead of the darkness of habit and conditioned beliefs. The second we decide to stand up for a Life on Purpose instead of falling into a Life in Default, in that moment we embrace the journey that life is and release the need for a specific destination. In reality, the destination is to become the highest expression of ourselves.

Love and Light,

Monique Moliere Piper

www.moniquemolierepiper.com